The truth about the rapture, tribulation, and Armageddon.

Leon Stewart

Copyright © 2000 by Leon Stewart. All rights reserved.

ISBN 0-939241-80-3

Author's Note

In the past few years, I have received numerous requests for copies of *Too Late*, which was first published in 1958. For that reason, I decided to offer this rewritten, updated version of the novel. Although the plot is the same, I have made some subtle theological changes.

Linda B. Jackson of Brewton, Alabama, has assisted me in this venture. Her creativity, her editorial ability, and her secretarial skills have contributed positively to the project.

May you, the reader, be blessed as you follow Joe and Sue through the pages of *Too Late*.

Leon Stewart

Too Late

by Leon Stewart

Set in small-town America, *Too Late* is a religious novel centered around the courtship and marriage of Joe Norton and Sue Martin. The story presents the infinite value of an older mentor, Shep Owen, sharing his business acumen with Joe as he establishes Norton's Auto Parts. It relates Joe's agony at his only sister's tragic death. It portrays the conflict within him after his self-defense slaying of a would-be rapist who is a common enemy to many of the local citizens. Involved in life's daily routine, Joe and Sue are astonished as the rapture of the Christian church takes place. The book details their survival during the tribulation period as outlined in the Revelation.

The novel depicts commitment and loyalty to Christ versus an independent desire to live in this world. Once a successful entrepreneur and the darling of his hometown, Joe's materialism evolves into an ugly spirit that tears him from those he loves, leaving only the will for self preservation. Sue's love for Joe remains overwhelming, but her devotion to Christ supersedes all other emotions. The drama climaxes with the Battle of Armageddon, which finds Joe and Sue on opposite sides.

Too Late will encourage the modern-day Christian to examine his own beliefs. Is moral goodness a ticket for the rapture? Will every believer be caught up in the rapture? Will anyone be converted during the tribulation period? These controversial issues are confronted in a riveting plot that grips the reader's attention to the last page.

TOO LATE

Chapter I

Given a knife, Joe Norton could have cut the tension that was suspended like a blanket over the booth where he sat with his dear friend and advisor, Shep Owen. Shep stared into his coffee as if the situation were as black as the contents of the cup. Joe was eager to know what was troubling Shep, but knew he would not speak until he was ready. As he waited, he looked around Johnny's Coffee Bar. Johnny was not in today, and Joe didn't know the new waitress. Most of the regular early-morning customers had already gone to their day's work.

Shep finally asked in a low, clear tone, "Joe, have you bought any parts from United Motor Parts?"

"Yes, about ten thousand dollars worth during the past three months." Joe's voice tightened because he almost knew what was coming next.

"Well, I want to warn you," continued Shep. "The company was a bogus one. They were stealing their merchandise from the government. Now that they have been caught, their customers will have to pay the government full price for all the parts."

"But I paid them cash already -- why must I pay again?" Joe interrupted.

"That's just it," Shep went on. "Those fellows are in jail and they can't pay. You know the government well enough to realize they will definitely get their money. Also, those fellows were underselling the value. I'd guess if you bought ten thousand dollars worth, it will cost you about eighteen thousand to get out of this."

Joe sat in silence. He had gone deep into debt to start his business. Norton's Motor Parts had been in operation only six months. Joe had finished college at State University and returned to his hometown of Winston to establish the business that had long been his dream. His father had assisted him, and Shep Owen, his friend and godfather, had helped build his business to a respectable volume. His stock was such that he had no competition within a seventy-five-mile radius. He was proud that every week since he had opened, revenues had increased over the prior week.

Yes, all had gone well, but this could prove a major setback. As Joe digested Shep's news, his face paled and his brown eyes hardened. The muscles in his jaw tightened, and fire raged in his bosom. He hated himself for becoming trapped in this!

"And what if I don't pay it?" he asked solidly.

Shep sighed. "You can't expect to beat the government, son. If it's on your books, you'll pay for it. Or they'll close your place and auction off your stock."

"If they do that, then what about the mortgage on the business? Will they pay it off?" Joe was greatly disturbed, but struggling for some answer to this dilemma.

"When they take over, it will be for their money. You will have to pay your honest debts, Joe." Shep's voice softened when he saw the despair in his young friend's face.

Joe's eyes flashed with an idea. "Shep, you said I'd have to pay for whatever is on my books. What if I take all that *off* my books before the auditors get here?"

Shep's eyes dropped to the table as he answered with a sharp rebuke. "I'm ashamed of you, Joe. If you do that, God will be against you. When He is not with you, the business will not prosper. I've always told you to be honest in all your dealings. If you are, son, then God will see you through. Besides, they have a list of everything. Joe, you know you cannot beat the government or the IRS. If what you purchased is not on your books, they may send you to the slammer for a while, boy."

Shep stopped, trying to read Joe's puzzled countenance. He had long ago realized that Joe possessed qualities that were scarce in the lives of most young men today -- character and determination. He knew Joe did not truly intend to pursue this alternative.

"Well, as far as I'm concerned, the government takes far too much from the working man. It's pay, pay, pay, and then pay some more! Even God requires only ten percent. What gives the IRS the right to take 30-40% of what I earn? It's just not fair!" His voice had risen angrily, and he pounded a fist on the tabletop.

Shep made no answer for he understood Joe was venting his frustration and helplessness. He sat in sympathetic silence until Joe muttered, "Okay, Shep. I'm sorry I went off on a tangent. But I hope you have a solution for me," said Joe wistfully.

"Get your books in order, Joe. The auditors will also check your taxes. When they tell you how much you owe, pay it," advised Shep.

"Pay it with what?" blurted Joe.

"Whatever you lack, I'll take care of it. You can repay me later. I will advise the bank to honor your check. Then I'll make a deposit to cover it," he talked quickly now.

"I can't do that," argued Joe. "You have been too good to me already. What if I can never repay you?"

Shep rose, saying, "Let's go, so you will have time to get your records in order. We cannot discuss every angle now, but I believe in you, son. And that's enough security for me."

Joe stood also and their eyes met. The tender gaze of the strong mechanic made a lump rise in Joe's throat. A tear threatened to surface, but he dared not let it. So many times Shep had been his confidant, his mentor, his support through trying circumstances.

"I'll succeed, Shep, just because of you." Joe blinked his eyes and started toward the door.

Joe was a stockily built man, strong and powerful. However, he was no match for Shep, who stood six feet and four inches and as straight as an arrow. His shoulders were broader than those of any other man in Winston. He tapered from his shoulders to his hips like a wedge. Though slightly gray around the temples, he had lost none of the vitality from the muscular body that bulged beneath his simple shop uniform. Yet in spite of this strength and the hard look on his face, Shep was as harmless as a kitten. His heart was much larger than his body, and the love within was extended to everyone with whom he came in contact. Especially to the young man who strolled beside him.

As they walked up the street, Shep knew all would be well now.

"Well, here comes Mr. Fisherman himself," called Ben Shank gaily, as Joe stepped inside Norton's Motor Parts. Almost everyone in Winston knew that Joe was an avid fisherman and often rose in the wee hours of the morning to fish a while before going to the store.

"Hello, Ben," responded Joe. He walked quickly behind the counter. "No fishing for me today. I've been visiting with Shep over at Johnny's. But I do appreciate your opening for me."

Ben Shank had been discharged from the Army three weeks before Norton's Motor Parts opened. Joe was glad when he secured Ben as his only employee. They had been close buddies in high school, and Joe knew Ben was competent and reliable. Ben had a powerful personality, and was always smiling and offering words of encouragement to the customers. He had contributed much to the rapid growth of Norton's Motor Parts, yet all the townspeople knew the backbone of the enterprise was the kind, courteous manner and the brilliant mind of Joe Norton.

Ben realized immediately that the visit with Shep had not been pleasant. The boss seemed enshrouded in thoughts that were almost as serious as death. He waited on a couple of customers who had entered the store, as Joe completed an order form and transmitted it by facsimile. Then Joe began looking through the morning tickets.

When the two customers left, Ben tried to lighten Joe's mood. "Northside Garage ordered parts totaling two thousand dollars on one purchase order this morning. And said they would call in another order within two weeks."

"Well, I'm thankful for that. But I've got a major problem, Ben, and I must ask for your help." He quickly related the situation, then both began working feverishly to get ready for the dreaded inspection. Neither of them stopped for lunch. At any moment the auditors might arrive, and if the books were not ready, the problem would be compounded.

At five-thirty that evening, Joe pulled the last report from the computer printer.

"You may leave, Ben, if you'd like. I believe everything's okay now. I'm going to stay a while longer." Joe double-checked his last total.

Ben rubbed his tired eyes and replied, "Okay, Joe. I'll go, but don't you worry about this. I'll stick with you, and if you need money, I'll help you get it."

"Thanks, Ben. I'll be all right. Please lock the door as you go." Joe had not told Ben about Shep's offer, but he truly appreciated his employee's loyalty.

"Uh-oh, I think we have company," Ben said, as he neared the front door.

Joe stood and looked through the huge plate-glass window. Two well-dressed men stepped through the doorway. One was short and stocky, with a broad face and a slim mustache. He wore a Hart Schaffner Marks suit and Bally shoes, but was somewhat homely. The other was taller and carried himself arrogantly. His face was sharp with narrow beady eyes, and it was obvious he considered himself an important person. His pinstriped suit was of equal quality to that of his associate.

"Good evening, sir," the taller man spoke.

"Good evening to you, gentlemen. May I help you?" This was Joe's usual greeting to a stranger.

The taller person presented his business card. He was Horace Longmeyer, a government inspector. Joe realized the purpose of the visit.

"Are you the proprietor here?" Longmeyer inquired.

"Yes, sir," Joe's reply was cool but not unfriendly.

"We are here to investigate any connection you may have with United Motor Parts." The more the taller man spoke, the more arrogant he seemed.

"Yes, I understand. I was expecting you." Joe tried to conceal his anxiety as he braced himself for the hours ahead.

"Who told you we would be here? Was it some of their men?" The shorter man, who had been introduced as Burton Talcott, spoke for the first time since the greeting.

"No, just a friend whose business you have already audited," responded Joe, as he reached for the page of figures he had just compiled.

"Do you mind if we check your books?" queried the mustached Talcott.

"Of course not, sir. I understand it would do no good to object." Joe beckoned them behind the counter and pointed toward the files.

"Will you need me, Joe?" asked Ben, who still stood where he had been when the inspectors had appeared.

"No, Ben. I'll see you in the morning. Remember to lock the door as you leave, please," replied Joe.

Ben locked the door and walked slowly across the street to his fire-engine red Mazda. Before pulling away from the curb, he glanced back into the store. The little guy had opened his briefcase and held many papers in his hand. The tall one was looking in the files. They were talking to each other, comparing papers, and making notes. Ben saw Joe standing by the counter with a worried expression on his tired face as he watched them.

"How I wish I could help him," Ben muttered as he accelerated the car and headed home.

Ben Shank was also well liked by everyone in Winston. Shortly after his tour with the Army, he had married Louise and they were now buying a home in a fashionable area of town. Ben drove five blocks north on Main Street, turned right at the United Methodist Church, and continued three blocks. He turned into the driveway of 301 Winchester Avenue and stopped at the door of his own garage. He stepped from the car and glanced toward the house. The three-bedroom, brick veneer, ranch style house was on a corner lot, and was attractive both inside and out.

As Ben stepped onto the sidewalk between Louise's well-tended flowerbeds, he felt the strain of the day and ached for some sympathy and rest. As his hand reached for the back door, it was opened from within and Louise greeted him with her usual "Hello, dear." He was amazed that these two simple words still sent a thrill through his heart.

"You must be a hungry man," said Louise, as she led him into the kitchen.

"Oh, I'm starved, but not too hungry to spend some time with my black-haired doll." Ben slipped his arm around her waist and lifted her into his arms. Though small in stature, Ben was a strong fellow.

"Oh, don't drop me, darling!" screeched Louise. "You always scare me when you do that." After a kiss, Ben lowered her gently to the floor. He stood in the kitchen a moment, admiring Louise's slim, graceful body that moved with the stealth of an Indian. Her soft black hair fell smoothly to her shoulders. Her long eyelashes, dark brows, and large hazel eyes had robbed Ben of his heart the first time he saw her.

"Honey, I'm almost jealous when I think about how beautiful you are," he commented.

Louise turned, blushing a bit. "Come, dear, and let's eat. You know my love is yours, and your happiness is mine forever."

Ben's expression changed as he sat across from her. Louise was a dedicated Christian who always gave thanks before every meal. Ben admired this, and for some time had shown an interest in her various church activities.

After the simple prayer, the meal was soon finished. They moved to the living room to relax and watch the evening news on television.

"I thought Joe might come over tonight. He hasn't been here in two weeks," remarked Louise.

"Oh, he had to stay at the store with a couple of inspectors." Ben didn't mention why the men had come. "He's a swell fellow, Louise, and as honest as anyone can be."

"Yes, he's been a friend to us, and I believe he'll really make good some day." Louise paused, as though in thought. "I wonder why he has not married. A wife could be a tremendous asset to him, and he seems settled enough to assume that responsibility."

"Joe is so caught up in his business that he doesn't think about such things, honey. But I imagine some girl will sweep him off his feet one day, just as you did me." Ben began to stroke Louise's hair.

Louise returned, "I don't think he would regret it, if he found the right girl. But we can't work out his life, so let's enjoy ours. Dear, are you going to church with me Wednesday night?"

"Yes. Your steadfast faith has almost persuaded me to become a Christian myself. I do believe it pays to serve God -- in this life and in the future."

"I'm sure of it, Ben. I'll be glad when you give your heart to God. Then I won't worry about you so much because God will take care of you." Louise was excited about the conversation because she had prayed since their wedding day that Ben would become a Christian.

For another hour they discussed church work and plans for their home, then Louise yawned. "Let's get to bed. Five o'clock comes mighty early."

"I'm with you, doll," said Ben, as he turned off the television.

On Tuesday morning before Joe unlocked the door of Norton's Motor Parts, he looked down the main thoroughfare of Winston. There were eight blocks in the business district. Main Street ran north and south, and Joe's place was located on the north end. He looked beyond the gray buildings to the park at the other end of town. Finally he glanced across the street to Winston Motors where Shep had been shop foreman for twelve years. Shep's ability as a mechanic was well respected in Winston. Joe wondered how Shep would feel when he learned how much the auditors' visit had cost him.

He reached for his key, unlocked the door, and stepped inside. As he turned on the lights, he murmured aloud, "I hope today will be much better than yesterday."

"How did it go last night?" asked Shep. He had been watching for Joe and had slipped in the door, unnoticed.

"Oh, hello, Shep. I guess it went okay. I had to spend eleven thousand dollars of your money. The amount due was eighteen thousand, and I had only seven." Joe was embarrassed as he spoke.

"Don't worry, son. I'll call the bank as soon as it opens. If you ever get the money, you can pay it back; if you don't, just accept it as a personal gift from a friend," replied Shep, as he came nearer to Joe.

"Oh, I'll repay you, Shep. You'll never know how much I appreciate your advice and assistance. If it hadn't been for you, I wouldn't be happy this morning." Joe glanced at the twenty-five rows of steel cabinets where thousands of parts were stocked. He shuddered as he thought of how close he had come to losing his business.

"Are you happy?" inquired Shep.

"You know I am, man. This is my dream, and if I lose it, I'd just as soon die." There was nothing but seriousness in Joe's voice, and Shep knew he spoke the truth.

"Well, I've got to get to work. You make a day of it, boy, and don't fret about this." Shep turned to go.

"Okay, Shep. See you soon," Joe called after him.

When Ben came in thirty minutes later, Joe discussed the previous night's events with him.

Shep Owen waved at a couple of friends as he watched for a chance to cross the street. Winston was a busy place today. In the past five years, prosperity had come to the town of approximately 16,000 residents. Of course, there had been prosperous years nationwide. The government had tried to plan so there would be no inflation of money. So far, these efforts had been successful, but almost everyone expected worse days to come.

When his chance came, Shep crossed the street, stepped over the curb to the sidewalk, and paused. His eyes narrowed to tiny slits as he observed the activity behind the large windows of Winston Motors. As the Chevrolet-Oldsmobile dealership, the business boasted an excellent reputation. Jack Drowd, the collection agent, and Oscar Morris, salesman for the company, were sitting close together. They apparently were discussing a matter of great importance.

Shep knew that Jack Drowd was a sneaking crook. He had served over four years in the penitentiary before being paroled ten years ago. It was beyond Shep why Mr. Shawn had hired Drowd, although he admitted Drowd had been a good collection agent to date. But he had worked against Shep in every way imaginable. Shep often desired to smash a fist into his repugnant face.

With his shoulders squared and his jaw set, Shep entered the front door. His eyes had turned to steel, and his soul told him he couldn't take anything off Jack Drowd today.

Oscar spoke first. "Good morning, Shep. You look rather sad. I'm sure everything will be okay."

Oscar was a pleasant man and a capable salesman. He had been with Winston Motors almost as long as Shep. Experience and adversity had welded the two men together. Drowd had tried for the past two years to turn short, rotund Oscar against Shep, but had been unsuccessful so far.

"Good morning, Oscar. I was just thinking -- nothing too serious, I suppose." Shep's words were frank. Although he and Oscar were friends, Oscar's association with Drowd did not erase Shep's suspicions about the man.

As Shep reached to open the doors from the showroom to the garage, Drowd spoke sarcastically. "Maybe you were thinking about Joe Norton and his slimy business across the street."

Actually, Drowd had desired to own such a business, but the laws did not permit it for a certain length of time after incarceration. He hated Joe and wanted to see him fail. He never missed an opportunity to malign Joe's name.

Shep turned a cold, marble-like face toward Drowd. The collection agent did not notice the expression in Shep's eyes, or he would not have continued.

"Oh, sure. Tell me that you would bash my brains out if you were not such a wonderful Christian. That's what the big, strong man always says," drawled Drowd. He fumbled nervously with a pencil. This was the boldest statement he had made to Shep.

Shep took two quick strides to the counter in front of Drowd. His long arm shot out, and his strong fingers clasped Drowd's necktie. The lightning speed of Shep's movements was too much for Drowd, and he could only hang stiffly in the grasp of the man he despised.

Shep's voice was bitter and cold. "Drowd, from this day forward, you'd better keep your nose out of my business and your tongue and hands off that boy and his business."

Drowd's lips snarled and his yellow teeth flashed. It had just dawned on him that he was the victim. Three mechanics had entered and stood watching the drama in disbelief. Oscar Morris had been too astonished to move. He remained in his swivel chair, his bald head glistening with perspiration like a freshly-peeled onion.

Drowd hissed, "And what if I don't, big boy?"

Fire boiled in the very soul of Shep Owen. He could tolerate Drowd's attacks on himself, but he could not bear it when they were turned on Joe Norton. He had invested more than money in that young man's future.

Drowd saw the anger in the foreman's eyes. He reached up and caught Shep's wrist. When he felt the powerful surge of muscle inside the sleeve of Shep's uniform, he realized he had gone too far. Color drained from his face, and sweat oozed from his forehead and ran down his cheeks. He opened his mouth to mutter an apology in order to save his skin, but he was one second too late.

Just as Drowd's lips parted, Shep pushed him to the full length of his left arm. His right fist, now like a war club, swung with power and speed. Drowd's hooked nose was a perfect target for the mighty blow.

Drowd saw the blow coming and tried unsuccessfully to dodge. He attempted to cry out, but the great force upon the bridge of his nose rendered him speechless. He felt sick in the pit of his stomach. He wanted to reach for something to hold onto, but his arms were useless. His vision was blurred, and a stream of crimson flowed swiftly over his upper lip. He fought the darkness that began to envelop him, but it was too great. As Shep's hand released his collar, he crumpled in a heap on the tile floor. It was a memorable sight indeed for anyone who might consider antagonizing Shep Owen.

For a second, Shep stared at the space where Drowd's head had been, then at the mass on the floor. When he turned back to Oscar, all the fire had burned out of him. He was again the Shep that Oscar had known for so long, except for a look of distress in his eyes. He spoke in a low tone, "Take care of things until I return, Oscar. Mr. Shawn won't be here today."

"Okay, Shep. Don't worry about this matter. I think you have just stopped a small cloud from becoming a storm." Oscar's voice was that of a friend, like oil in a wound to Shep.

"Thanks, Oscar. Boys, you may go to your work. I won't be there for a while." It was the first time Shep had noticed the three spectators.

He walked to his car and was soon driving north on Main Street. Five blocks later he pulled to the curb and stepped out. He looked at the huge building before him.

When he saw the towering steeple, the bulletin board, and the eleven steps leading to the entrance, he knew this was a safe refuge for him. He dearly loved his church.

Shep did not fear the law. Drowd would not dare mention their encounter, since he was on parole. But he did fear the invisible hand of a loving, yet just, God. Now his thoughts were only of God, and he felt this was the best place in the world to find Him.

He pushed on the heavy oak door, which was always unlocked for those who wished to enter and pray. As he went into the sanctuary from the vestibule, his eyes were drawn to the choir loft. Behind it was a picture of Jesus Christ weeping over Jerusalem. It seemed to Shep that this Christ, who loved him so much, was weeping over him now. He bowed his head and a tear splashed softly on the crimson carpet. Shep lifted his head and looked again. Jesus seemed to stretch forth compassionate arms to the distraught man and to say, "My son, if you are heavy laden, come unto Me, and I will give you rest."

The bitterness passed from the kind foreman's heart. The horrible nightmare was over. Through eyes half blinded by tears, he searched for the door of the men's prayer room. He had been there many times, and now he walked by instinct down the long aisle. He turned left in front of the altar, and passed through an open door.

After closing the door, Shep wiped his eyes and looked about the room. It was very familiar, for he had often poured out his heart to God here. Just as often, he had found rest, peace, and contentment for his soul. There were three chairs around a table, upon which lay an open Bible. Underneath a large picture of Jesus Christ praying in the Garden of Gethsemane, there were two pews.

Shep sat down and began reading in the Bible. He behaved as though someone else was in the room, and indeed, there was. The presence of the Lord comforted His troubled child, saying, "Don't worry, son. I am with you always, even unto the end of the world."

For over an hour, Shep was lost in the serene, fascinating power of the Word. The Word is sharp, and Shep had already felt its chastisement in his soul. He closed the Bible and knelt beside one of the pews. For a long moment, he bowed in silence, then he prayed aloud. "Oh, God, the thing I have greatly feared has come upon me. But I know You will not forsake me, even in this hour of distress."

Ben entered the store at eleven-forty-five. He always left for lunch at eleven, and usually returned five or ten minutes past twelve. He was accompanied today by his wife Louise.

"What are you celebrating today, boy?" asked Joe, looking at the clock on the wall, then at Ben. He had not expected his employee back so soon.

"You might know something is up," Ben grinned. "Louise is going to Conway to shop, so she rushed me back here today." He looked lovingly at Louise.

"Hi, Louise," greeted Joe.

"Hello, Joe. I wanted to see if you needed something from Conway before I go. Mother is going with me, and I'll be glad to pick up anything you say."

Joe thought briefly, then picked up his pen. As he wrote, he said, "I'll tell you what, Louise. I'll fax an order to Grover's Place. You can pick it up for me before you return, please."

"I'll be happy to do that," stated Louise as she pulled out her memo pad and made a note. "Anything else?"

"No, I guess not," replied Joe, thumping the counter as though that stimulated his thinking.

"I'll be going then." She smiled at Ben and teased, "I'll try not to spend all our money. Bye, dear."

Ben leaned forward and kissed her gently on the mouth. "Bye, doll. You get whatever you want. Be sure to get the fabric for the drapes, too."

As Louise walked to the door, both men admired her graceful carriage. One admired her because she belonged to him, and his love for her was greater than that for his own life. The other admired her, as did the rest of the town, for her devotion to her husband and to her God. It was not unusual to see married women who were too friendly with other men. But everyone in Winston respected Louise. Joe watched her get in the car. Her green silk blouse complemented her plaid skirt perfectly. "She always dresses so attractively," he thought.

As he stood there considering Louise's beauty and her loyalty to Ben, he exclaimed, "I sometimes wish I had a wife like yours, Ben!"

Ben turned to his work, then remarked, "Joe, I also wish you had a good wife. It would mean a lot to have someone to talk to and share things with, someone who is really interested in you."

"Oh, I don't guess there's a girl in this world for me, Ben. But no need dwelling on that, so I'll go eat. I'll see you after a bit." As Joe started toward the door, his dream of a wife had already vanished.

"You going home for lunch?" asked Ben.

"No, I'm going to walk to Suzie's. She told me yesterday that she would have roast beef and sweet potatoes, so I'm headed that way." This was Joe's favorite meal and Suzie knew it. The two were friends and she always let Joe know when his favorite foods would be on the menu.

"Don't eat too much," called Ben, as Joe left the store.

As Joe walked the two blocks to Suzie's, he greeted all the people he met. He spoke to the merchants who stood in their doorways and to old friends across the street. He knew almost everyone, and they knew and liked him.

When he entered Suzie's place, he realized it was packed, as usual. He spoke to those he knew nearest the door. Some he didn't know, but all were engaged in devouring the delicious food Suzie's cooks had prepared. Joe scanned the crowd for an empty booth, but all were taken. He heard a familiar voice at his elbow.

"Hello, fisherman. You want something to eat?" He turned to see Suzie close by. She was middle aged, a little stout, dressed in her usual uniform of black slacks and white blouse. Her coal black hair was pulled back from her face, which glowed with a wholesome, friendly smile. She had such an outgoing, non-judgmental personality that she was like a second mother to many of the young people of Winston.

"Who told you I was fishing?" Joe asked.

"Everyone knows the Norton boy is rich and that he likes to fish." Both laughed at Suzie's remark. She was always "carrying on" good naturedly with Joe.

"There's no place for me to sit, so I guess I'll go somewhere else," murmured Joe, as he continued to search the booths.

Suzie leaned closer and whispered, "I've got a special piece of beef saved for you, boy, and you're not going anywhere." Joe smiled at her.

Then Suzie said, "Come with me. I'll find you a seat."

Joe followed her to the rear of the crowded restaurant. As they went, she apologized, saying funny things to the people who had to move to let them pass. In the back of the room, Suzie stopped at the last booth, and asked, "Sue, would you mind letting a young man share this booth with you?"

"Of course not," answered a voice Joe had never heard. From where he stood, he could not see who had spoken.

Suzie turned to Joe, "Sit here, and I'll serve your plate."

Joe pushed by the last chair, excusing himself, and eased into the booth. His back was toward the rear wall. The music box stood beside this booth, almost concealing it from the rest of the restaurant.

"Hello," said the girl across from him.

Joe looked at her and all rationale deserted him. He met the gaze of two dark blue eyes set in the oval face of a striking blonde. To his dismay, he felt himself blush slightly. "Hello. I believe Suzie said your name is Sue."

"Yes, I'm Sue Martin."

"I'm glad to meet you. I am Joe Norton," responded Joe, admiring her face and wondering if the rest of her looked as good. She wore a red tee shirt under a blue denim jumper that emphasized the sapphire of her eyes.

Sue's eyebrows arched slightly and her brow wrinkled. "Are you the owner of Norton's Motor Parts?"

"Yes, I hang out there most of the time." Joe smiled broadly. It always thrilled him when someone connected him with the store. Especially someone as attractive as this young woman.

"Well, I'm certainly honored. The first time I eat out in Winston, I get to eat with one of the businessmen." Sue noticed his handsome features as she talked. His dark brown hair was neatly cut, but a lock of it often fell forward slightly onto his forehead. His eyes were a warm brown and conveyed honesty and open admiration. He wore casual slacks and a sport shirt open at the neck. Sue observed he wore no wedding band, then immediately scolded herself silently for noticing.

"Are you a newcomer to Winston?" questioned Joe, as he sipped the glass of water before him.

"We've been here four months. My father transferred to the pulp mill here from Semach. I am a nurse, and I began a job at General Hospital last week. I was shopping today and decided to lunch here. Suzie has been very cordial and the food is delicious." Sue gestured toward her near-empty plate.

Suzie broke into the conversation with a big laugh. She held a plate piled with roast beef and sweet potatoes. "Even better than your mother fixes them, Joe. And you eat every bit."

Joe looked at the plate, then at Suzie. "That looks wonderful. I'll certainly do it justice. And, Suzie, thanks for securing me a place in this booth today." He looked at Sue as he made the last statement.

Suzie smiled as she looked at the blushing young woman. "Joe is one of the grand young fellows of Winston, Sue. You'll make a hit with everyone in town if you can make one with him." She walked away, grinning broadly, and very pleased with herself.

"Suzie is truly a fine person, and her life is a long, interesting story. Maybe I can tell it to you some day." Joe began to eat.

"Everyone I have met here seems nice, and I do like this town," commented Sue, as she began to eat her dessert.

"It's the greatest. Because the people are usually in a hurry, it often seems they are interested only in themselves. But they do love one another." Joe paused and reflected seriously a minute, then continued. "This generation is a very selfish one. People often disagree and fight over such insignificant matters."

"You are so right," agreed Sue. "I wish people would be more Christ-like and love each other as He loves us. It would be a wonderful world."

There was a lull in the conversation and Joe continued eating. Sue had finished, but the company was so stimulating that she had remained. Not only was this Joe Norton a well-known businessman, but he seemed to be a man of good morals and he possessed a winning personality.

Sue broke the silence. "Mr. Norton, do you go to church?"

Joe hesitated, his eyes downcast. His people were churchgoers, but he had been so engrossed in his work that he felt he had no time for it. He wanted to avoid answering this question. It was evident to him that Sue was a devout Christian. Finally, he replied shamefacedly, "No, I don't. I know I should, but I've always figured I was too busy."

"That's what is wrong with this country," Sue stated bluntly. "Mr. Norton, people should take time to go to church and to worship God." Joe detected an eagerness in her voice, and he found himself admiring this trait. Joe knew many church attendees who did not live up to biblical doctrines. But here was a Christian he believed in, although their acquaintance was very short.

"It appears you have more enthusiasm for the church than most folks," observed Joe.

Sue refused to accept the flattery. "No, it isn't just enthusiasm. It's the love of Christ and a burden for lost humanity. That's what makes me want to see the church go forward. I wish everyone was faithful to God and to His church." She paused, analyzing her next words. "But everyone will not be faithful in carrying out God's will. So it doesn't pay to look at others. We must keep our eyes on Christ. He will never fail us."

These statements sank into Joe's heart. Not only had the message been powerful, but the messenger talked as if she genuinely loved the church. He told himself she must surely be the most remarkable Christian he had ever met.

When he spoke again, Joe was very serious. "I've wanted to go to church for a long time, but I've just neglected it. I know it's right. I have many friends who attend Winston Community Church on North Main Street. I think I would be there Sunday morning if I had the right encouragement from a certain person I have met recently."

Sue studied his face intently and believed his words. Her voice became warm and tender. "That person would like you to go to church every Sunday."

Joe's eyes met the full gaze of the sapphire eyes across the table. He felt they saw more than the ordinary people whom Joe dealt with every day. They penetrated his dignity and delved into his soul. As Sue's voice snapped him out of his trance, he reassured himself this was no dream.

"I need to go home and get some rest," she said, collecting her few small packages and rising.

"I have to get back to work myself. I may get fired for being thirty minutes late, but it has been worth it," added Joe, walking beside her to the cashier.

"That was a delicious meal, Suzie," complimented Sue, receiving her change.

"Thank you, dear. Come back when you can." Suzie spoke in a motherly voice.

"Yes, the food was good, and I'll not forget this meal as long as I live," said Joe, glancing meaningfully from Suzie to Sue.

"Didn't I tell you a month ago that I was looking out for you, boy?" laughed Suzie. Joe heartily agreed, but Sue smiled only faintly. Though all the other diners had left, she was somewhat embarrassed.

"May I use your phone to call a taxi?" she asked Suzie.

"Surely, but they're probably all busy this time of day. Try 526-4978," advised Suzie.

Joe interrupted, "If you will permit me, I'll drive you home. My car is just up the street a couple of blocks." He was nervous, unsure that she would accept. And Joe hated to be the loser in anything.

Sue hesitated, her hand on the phone. "I thought you had to get back to work."

"Oh, that's not important when a young lady is in need," replied Joe, his eyes twinkling. He looked directly at her, as though willing her to say 'yes.'

Blushing again, she turned to the door and said, "I don't know why, but I believe I will accept your offer, Mr. Norton."

"See you later, Suzie," called Joe. And he exited, beautiful Sue by his side.

The town had returned to its usual hum of business as the couple walked along the sidewalk. A few folks noticed Joe and Sue, but they had things on their minds other than getting a joke on Joe. Soon they came to the big store that had almost a solid glass front. A large sign hung over the walk "Norton's Motor Parts."

"This must be your store," assumed Sue, reading the sign.

"Yes, it is. Ben seems rather busy, but he'll make out until I get back. Here's my car." Joe hoped his employee wouldn't look out and see him now because he knew Ben would tease him unmercifully.

Joe opened the car door, and Sue slipped onto the soft seat of Joe's new Oldsmobile. He had secured this car through Shep shortly after he had opened his business. It was the creamy color of buttermilk, and he was very proud of it.

"Say you live on Main Street?" asked Joe.

"Yes. A half-mile past the church. I'll show you. It's in the country, but that's what Dad likes."

"I'm a country boy, too. My father is a farmer, and his place is two miles beyond the school," said Joe, as he drove north on Main Street.

"I know you're really proud of your business," commented Sue.

"Yes, but I hope we can expand our radius of coverage. I think I've got a system in place now that will bring additional business from nearby towns." Sue could hear the pride in his voice.

"I'm sure your business will grow, but I hope you don't keep thinking you're too busy for church. I have met your parents and they seem delightful. Your sister Ann and I are in the same Sunday School class. She's been very friendly and seems a good Christian. It would be so nice if you came with them each Sunday." Joe could hear the enthusiasm in her voice.

"So you've already met my family. They are fine folks. Dad is responsible for my having my business.

He and Mother are both very good to me, and my sister is my closest friend. She's about the only girl I ever take anywhere. If she wants anything, I want her to have it, even if I have to sacrifice." It was well known in Winston that the Nortons were a close-knit family.

"Did you say your dad's a farmer?" asked Sue.

"Yes, he has a large farm out -- say, that's Shep's car at the church. Wonder what he's doing there this time of day." Joe slowed the car to a crawl, curious about Shep. He had no idea Shep was in great agony because of him.

The affair between Shep and Jack Drowd had not been spread by the witnesses, so Joe had not heard about it. It was kept quiet because of the two parties involved. For Drowd, because it might mean a return to prison; for Shep, because he was so respected by the men and they didn't want people talking about their foreman.

"Who is Shep?" questioned Sue, looking first at Shep's car, then at the church.

"Shep Owen. He's the shop foreman at Winston Motors. He's also a member of Winston Community Church and one of the best fellows in this country. He's been a fine friend to me. I'm tempted to stop, but he may be busy or want to be alone." Joe stepped on the gas.

"Oh, I know Mr. Owen," said Sue. "He's the head usher at church. He surely is a big and rough-looking man to be so kind and courteous."

"Shep wouldn't hurt a thing. He's everybody's friend," answered Joe. If only he knew how badly Shep had hurt the nose of Jack Drowd only a few hours before.

For several moments, only the hum of the car's engine was heard. They had passed the city limits sign and on either side of the road were fields of corn almost ready for harvest. Both Joe and Sue were a little uneasy, though each had decided it was exciting to be in the company of the other.

Finally, Joe mustered up his courage and asked, "Sue, will you go out with me tomorrow night? We could have dinner, then go for a ride and talk about this town and its people -- and about you."

"But you don't go out with any girls except your sister," teased Sue.

Joe looked at her broad smile, then both laughed happily.

"Well," drawled Joe, "I'm old enough to break away from Sis. And she won't mind when I tell her I'm going with you." He felt he had almost won Sue's confidence.

"Tomorrow is Wednesday, and that's about the only night I go out during the week. But it's prayer service at church, and I couldn't miss it," advised Sue.

"Are you saying I could take you to church tomorrow night?" Joe stole a glance at the silky blond hair about her shoulders.

"Oh, there's my house on the right," exclaimed Sue, as they neared a small white bungalow which sat fifty feet off the highway.

Joe turned into the driveway. When he opened the car door for Sue, she stood a moment looking into his handsome face.

"If it's a deal that I take you to church tomorrow night, then maybe we could have dinner together before we go," suggested Joe.

Sue looked thoughtfully across the open field as she wondered whether to accept his invitation. Joe had been so kind, so interesting.

"All right, Mr. Norton. I'll be ready at six o'clock. That will give us over an hour to eat before the service." Her voice lowered. "I hope I'm not doing the wrong thing."

"Look, I call you 'Sue' and it would please me if you would call me 'Joe.' And don't worry. I would not do anything to separate you from your God. Truly I believe as you do, even if I am not as good as you." Joe's voice was strong and clear, and he leaned earnestly toward Sue.

She pushed a lock of hair from her forehead. She hesitated a moment longer, then replied, "Okay . . . Joe. I'll see you." With these words, she turned and walked into the house without looking back.

Joe watched her trim figure pass through the doorway, then drove quickly to the store. He found Ben busy with customers and telephone inquiries.

"My, you surely must have eaten plenty today," he drawled, as Joe came behind the counter.

"Well, the future will probably reveal a lot," hinted Joe, with a smile.

Even though it was Tuesday evening, the boys had as much business as they could handle. Both worked diligently to satisfy the customers, because they realized Norton's Motor Parts was under a great debt now which must be paid.

Ben left the store at five-thirty. He went straight home to enjoy the delicious hot meal Louise had prepared and to spend a relaxing evening with her.

Joe stayed at the store until six, then drove to his home where he lived with his parents and sister Ann. The 4,000-acre farm was one of the largest in Lincoln County. Joe parked in the double garage, then walked leisurely into the house. His parents were seated at the supper table.

"Hello, son," came the pleasant voice of Mrs. Norton.

"Good evening, son," greeted his dad.

"Hello, Mother. Hi, Dad. How are you two?"

"We're fine, Joe. How was business today?" asked Mr. Norton.

"The best we've had in many days," answered Joe, as he sat down at the table. "Where's Ann?"

"She's gone to the store for some chocolate. She intends to prove to you that she can make fudge." Mrs. Norton smiled.

"That girl is a sight," replied Joe, as he began to eat the soup his mother had set before him.

"We started gathering the corn today, son. I believe we'll get a better yield than I expected." Mr. Norton reached for a toothpick.

"I'm sure your yield will be greater than anyone else's around here. And your corn's the prettiest, too, Dad." Joe truly admired his father.

Mr. Norton was in his early fifties, with slightly gray hair. He was well respected and was a deacon at Winston Community Church on North Main. He loved God first and foremost. Next to God, he revered his home. He and Mrs. Norton had been married for twenty-six years. He had sent Joe to college and established him in business. At present, he was trying to give Ann a good education and let her choose a vocation. However, his love for his family did not exceed their reciprocal love and admiration.

"Well, hello, big shot," quipped Ann, bursting through the door behind Joe and slapping him on the shoulder.

"Hi, schoolgirl," he returned. "What are you up to tonight?"

"I learned a new recipe today and I thought I'd try it on you. I know you think few girls are learning to cook these days, but I'm going to prove you wrong," laughed Ann, reaching for a pan.

"I'll help you, so we can be sure it will be tasty," teased Joe, rising from the table.

"She'll need some help," laughed Mrs. Norton, as she began to clear the dishes.

"All right, Mother. You and Daddy may laugh now, but I will learn to cook," replied Ann.

"That's right, dear. You become an excellent cook like your mother, and I'll be proud of you," placated Mr. Norton. "I'm going to read the newspaper and get to bed. It's been a hard day for me, and I have to get up earlier than you two."

"You should stay up long enough to eat some candy," said Ann.

"Oh, I'll get some in the morning," promised Mr. Norton.

Ann, Mrs. Norton, and Joe were soon busy, with Mrs. Norton serving as instructor. She was an attractive woman, although her health had begun to fail in the past three years. She never complained, but the family had noticed she was unable to do much work. She soon removed her apron, and said, "Children, I think I'll leave you now and get to bed. I need to help your daddy tomorrow." She left the kitchen.

"Joe, I want to use your car on Christmas Eve," requested Ann.

"Why, it's three months until Christmas, and a lot could happen between now and then," laughed Joe.

"Seriously, I have to know if I can use it so I can make plans."

"You may if you'll be back by the time I close the store," said Joe, after thinking a minute.

"Oh, I'll be back early in the afternoon. Several of us girls are planning to lunch together after spending the morning in something that is a secret," responded Ann, pouring the fudge onto a platter.

"My, I wonder if that will be edible." Joe grinned at his sister.

"It certainly smells wonderful," commented Ann, as she placed the candy in the refrigerator.

"Let's play Trivial Pursuit while the candy hardens," suggested Ann.

"Okay, it's still early and I've nothing else to do. You get the board, and I'll beat you in a game," teased Joe.

"Who said you can beat me?" retorted Ann, bringing the game and joining him at the table.

"Are you sure no boys are going with you girls on Christmas Eve?" Joe was in a mood to aggravate tonight.

"Of course, I'm sure! I wouldn't spoil our plans by including any boy." Ann blushed. "Are you sure I can borrow your car?"

"Of course, if you have it back by six."

"Why are you so eager to have it back by then?" asked Ann.

"Oh, you'll find out soon enough. It's your turn," answered Joe.

The game was over an hour later and they ate delicious, pecan-filled, chocolate fudge.

"I'm going to bed," Joe yawned, "before I see you make yourself sick."

"No way, Joe. And you ate far more than I did. You'll probably not be able to sleep, since I beat you soundly at Trivial Pursuit," taunted Ann.

"Oh, I'll beat you next time, little sister. And leave some of that fudge for Mother and Dad," said Joe gaily, as he left the kitchen.

"This is my last piece. I'm headed for bed, too. See you tomorrow evening."

Business was fair at Norton's Motor Parts on Wednesday. At five minutes past twelve, big Shep Owen pulled up in his white AstroVan.

"Say, Joe, could I interest you in taking the afternoon off and riding up to Little River to watch me catch a fish?"

Ben said to Joe, "Go ahead, Joe. I can handle the store this afternoon."

"What time will you have me back?" Joe asked Shep.

"What difference will it make, boy? You have until seven o'clock in the morning," said Shep loudly.

"Oh, no, he hasn't," chimed in Ben. "He's got a date with some little girl tonight."

"I don't believe it," remarked Shep. "There's not a girl in Winston who would go out with him."

Shep and Ben often teased Joe, but Joe was a good sport. He laughed as the two men looked questioningly at him.

"Who is she, Ben?" Shep questioned.

"I don't know, and he won't tell me." This sent Shep and Ben into hearty guffaws again.

"You guys will find out soon enough," Joe advised, wondering if Ben had seen him with Sue on Tuesday.

"We'll be back pretty early, Joe. I've got some work at home to do, and it's prayer meeting night," informed Shep.

"Okay. Where will you pick me up?" asked Joe.

"Drive your car to my place and let's eat a bite there. Your rod and reel are at my house, anyway. Then we'll head straight to Little River."

"Okay," agreed Joe. He said to Ben, "And thanks, Ben, for being willing to tend the store alone this afternoon."

Shep and Joe turned their cars onto Second Street, drove for one-half mile, took a left, and entered Shep's driveway.

"Say, you've been doing some more work around here, haven't you?" asked Joe, as he exited the car and looked about him.

"Yes. A fellow worked in the yard a couple of days last week and really made a difference."

The house was in a lovely location and was well constructed. It was a long, ranch style, brick home. Shep had built it three years earlier, and the lawn had recently been landscaped. The two friends walked inside and Shep called, "Are you asleep, honey?"

"No, dear, I'm here," replied a soft, clear voice.

"Come and see who's with me. Sit down, Joe." Shep walked toward another room.

"Oh, I imagine I know who it is," answered Mrs. Owen, coming through the doorway. "Hello, son. How are you? It's been a while since I saw you." She smiled at Joe.

Mrs. Owen was lovely. She was forty-eight years old, with some gray in her black hair. She was always tender and affectionate. Her face was bright, and she often wore a happy smile. The entire town admired her kindness and consideration for others. Five years earlier, she and Shep had been in an automobile accident. Shep was not seriously hurt, but Mrs. Owen's back was broken and her spine injured. She was hospitalized four months, and then came home in a wheelchair. She was paralyzed from her waist down, and her chair was her only means of getting about the house. Now she talked to Joe as if he were her own son.

He took her extended hand, and pressed it gently in his own. "I'm doing fine. We've been busy lately. But how are you? People often ask me about you."

"I'm okay, Joe. Though I am still in this wheelchair, I believe God will heal me one day and make me a living testimony of his miracle-working power."

Since the accident, she had firmly believed she would walk again. Her faith never wavered, and Joe knew she clung to the promises of God -- the same promises that his own mother had told him so much about.

"Yes, I believe you will walk again, too, Mrs. Owen."

"Is anything ready to eat, dear?" asked Shep. "Joe and I are going fishing for a while."

"Yes, Mamie left lunch on the stove. I'll put it on the table, and you two can eat. I know you're anxious to tease the fish." Mrs. Owen wheeled herself toward the kitchen.

As she was hindered in her housework, Mamie Blackwell had been hired as their maid. She had been a faithful employee for the past four years.

"We may fool one into the boat today," laughed Shep. He and Mrs. Owen often teased each other like children.

"Oh, I'm sure you will," conceded Mrs. Owen, as she put the food on the table.

Soon they had eaten and were on their way to the river. The autumn evening was a bit cool for many fishermen, but for these two, it was perfect.

Fifteen miles out of Winston, Shep turned right onto a gravel road, drove another mile, then parked at the boat landing of Little River State Park.

"Well, here it is," announced Joe happily, as he sprang from the car and looked over the lake.

"Yes, and it's nice and calm. The fish should bite today," observed Shep, as he and Joe unloaded the fishing gear.

It was a beautiful park. The grass and shrubbery were well tended. Picnic grounds covered the hillside behind them. There was a concession stand to their left, and far up the hillside were several tourist cabins. The lake lay clear and still, as placid as glass. It was about a mile wide with green growth decking its banks. A pier ran from the concession stand about fifty feet into the water, and on it was a large platform. In the center of this swimming area were two diving boards. Joe had dived from that platform many times, but he stood awed at the beauty before him. He observed the smooth lake, then his gaze went to the spillway where water poured gently over the dam to dash angrily at the rocks, then rush madly on its course.

"This water reminds me of life, Shep," he mused aloud. "Some things are calm like the lake. Others are exactly opposite, like the water after it goes over the dam."

"How is that?" asked Shep, looking over the lake.

"Well, you see how smooth it is there, then how it becomes so angry as it goes over the spillway." Joe talked very seriously, as he put the equipment into the boat and climbed in.

"Yes, son. We never know what obstacles we must face, but if God is with us, we shall never fall on the rocks as angrily as the water does. That's why I pray so often that you will give your heart and life to God soon." His skillful hands fastened the motor to the boat.

Joe looked at the sky, then into the water, before replying. "I do plan to start going to church soon, Shep."

Shep recognized the soberness of Joe's voice but didn't answer. He felt certain the Spirit of God had touched the heart of his young friend by his illustration.

As the caretaker of the park was well acquainted with Shep, he permitted him to put his own boat into the lake. The two men were silent as they sped toward the river. They were always at ease with each other, whether talking or silent.

About a hundred feet into the river, Shep stopped the motor and paddled the boat quietly and slowly until they were near the east bank. Both men began casting. After an hour, Shep had caught a fine bass. Joe worked hard trying to reel one in and put an end to Shep's teasing.

"Well, I just don't think it's meant for me to catch anything today," grumbled Joe.

"I think you're working at it too hard. Or maybe you're too excited," laughed Shep.

"You may be right." He placed his reel in the bottom of the boat. "Are the cokes in the ice chest?"

"Yes. Bring me one while I catch another fish," said Shep, feigning an air of pride.

Joe opened two drinks and handed one to Shep without a word. He sat at the bow of the boat, drinking his coke and staring deeply into the water.

"What are you doing, Joe -- trying to conjure one up?" asked Shep.

"No, I was thinking about Ben. What's wrong with him these days?" Joe picked up his reel again.

Shep was silent a moment, then talked thoughtfully. "I don't exactly know, Joe, but I think he may be having some problems at home."

"You don't mean with Louise!" exclaimed Joe.

"No, Louise is a remarkable Christian girl. I believe the trouble lies within Ben himself."

"I don't understand," Joe said in a puzzled tone.

"Well, Louise is a beautiful girl and has six blue ribbons from beauty contests to prove it." Shep paused, then continued. "Many, many years ago, she had a secret friendship that few people knew about. Ben got wise to it before they married, and she stopped it. However, I think now he is trying to bring it all up again. I know that Louise has been true to Ben since they married." Shep turned and cast toward the bank.

"Who was this secret friend, Shep?" inquired Joe, baiting his line.

A shadow passed over Shep's face. He had dreaded this question. But there were no secrets between these two, and Shep hissed his answer. "Jack Drowd."

"Drowd!" exclaimed Joe. He turned to Shep, his face twisted in horror. He saw that Shep sat as solid as iron, with fire in his eyes and a jaw like chiseled marble. Joe had never seen Shep look so angry. He demanded, "Tell me about it."

"There's no need to discuss the past too much, Joe. Drowd told me about it. He showed me things back then that proved their association. It is a dark time in Louise's life that she would like to blot out, but which can never be undone."

Both men fished in silence. Joe was weighing this news in his mind, while Shep wondered how Joe would take this information about his friend and employee.

Shep spoke again. "Joe, those things are in the past. Louise has become a Christian, and she is making Ben a fine wife. I'm sure the mistake hurt her more than anyone else, and Ben should understand that."

He continued, "Joe, this illustrates why I talk to you so much, son. Some events in our lives are not so easily overcome. Their effects often reach far beyond the present to haunt us in the future. There are things you could do now that would create painful memories for you in years to come." Shep spoke softly.

"I know you're right, Shep, and I want to do my best. But let's not talk about such unpleasantness any more. If the worst develops, we must help Ben and Louise." Joe realized the disaster that might be pending for the young couple whom he dearly loved.

"I'll do all I can, Joe," assured Shep. "But let me mention one more item before we close the subject. What started Ben on this spree was that the other day at the shop, Jack Drowd bragged that he had been with, or could go with, any woman in Winston."

Joe's eyes flashed as he thought of two girls -- his sister Ann and Sue Martin. "There are some girls he will never go with in this town," he blurted.

"Certainly that's true. But Drowd was just taunting Ben, and Ben knows what a convincing Romeo he is."

"He'll be a dead Romeo if he fools with some girls in Winston," shouted Joe.

"Don't worry, Joe. Drowd's just a big bluff," soothed Shep.

"Hey, I've got one!" yelled Joe. "He must be a whopper!" He stood and reeled in a three-pound bass.

"He is a fine one," admired Shep, after the fish was safe in the net.

"Now who's the best fisherman out here?" teased Joe.

"Hey, the evening is not over yet," reminded Shep.

"I don't know about that. It's four o'clock, and I need to go." Joe was thinking about his plans for the evening. His anger was gone, and he felt happy as they motored back to the landing. It was seldom that he landed a larger fish than Shep caught. But his thoughts were on a lovely girl who had to be at work at ten o'clock tonight.

"And I get to pick her up at six o'clock and be with her until I take her to work at ten," he murmured to himself.

"What did you say?" yelled Shep, over the roar of the motor.

Joe grinned at him. "Nothing, fisherman. Nothing at all."

Chapter II

After closing the store Wednesday afternoon, Ben Shank drove furiously toward his home. He wanted to be alone with his own worries. For several days, he had not been himself. He was usually jolly and teasing, but lately he had been extremely moody. He hated himself for allowing Jack Drowd's boastful words to torment him. Since Drowd had been in Norton's Motor Parts a week ago, Ben had heard his taunting remarks ringing in his ears almost constantly. "I can go with <u>any</u> girl in Winston, married or unmarried, if I set my mind to it." And Drowd had sneered at Ben when he said it, causing Ben to remember the painful night that Louise had told him of her past relationship with Drowd. It wasn't that Ben didn't trust Louise. He did. And he knew she had been true to him. But Ben also knew how winsome and persistent Drowd could be. All of Winston had seen Drowd work his evil magic on several girls since his release from prison.

Joe had observed his employee's bad humor, and it had worried him, for he thought Ben might be dissatisfied with his job. The customers had noticed, too, and had remarked to Joe about the sour disposition Ben had developed. Ben had once been the life of the store and had brought cheer and encouragement to the customers, but no longer. More than anyone else, Louise had noticed it and had spent much time in prayer about it.

Ben pulled his Mazda into his driveway, stepped out, and slammed the door disgustedly. He walked through the back door where Louise waited as usual to greet him warmly.

"Hello, dear," she whispered softly and lovingly.

"Hello," Ben replied, and kissed her lightly on the cheek -- more for the purpose of getting her out of his path than anything else.

Louise sensed this, and her face twisted with pain. Though her heart was torn, she pretended she had not perceived any difference in her husband. "Dinner is ready, honey," she said, as she turned to hide a couple of tears.

Ben went to the bathroom and washed his hands without speaking another word. Why these misunderstandings had come to their home, Louise could not fathom. But she believed God would work things out, if the two of them would allow His intervention.

Louise had been a wonderful cook, even before they married. The meal was delicious, but because of Ben's attitude and Louise's desire to resolve the matter, very little food was eaten.

Ben ate in silence. When he finished, he pushed his plate back and stared into space. He felt guilty about his behavior toward Louise, but some evil force within him urged him to vent his frustrations upon the woman he loved more than anything or anyone else on earth.

Louise interrupted his thoughts. "Would you like some dessert, dear?"

"No, I don't believe so," Ben responded sullenly.

"Ben." There was a different tone in Louise's voice. It was trembling, yet carried a forceful note. Ben looked into her face and knew what was coming next. He wished he could avoid this unpleasantness, yet he knew his heart would not rest until the problem was discussed.

"Yes?" he asked reluctantly.

"I wish we could talk. Whatever is bothering you is my concern, too. I am interested in our home and in our future. We cannot continue to treat each other as we have for the past several days."

It was an earnest appeal for him to confide in her. How could he refuse such a sweet, unselfish wife? But Ben didn't answer. He just sat, looking into her face.

Louise began again, "Darling, you know that I love you and want to help you. There are only two desires in my heart. The first is to serve God and please Him. The second is to make you happy and to please you. When I fail in either endeavor, then my life becomes lonely and miserable."

She paused, then, "What is the matter, Ben?"

For a long moment, Ben continued to sit in silent thought. When he spoke, he was slow and deliberate. "Well, I guess it's all something in my mind, Louise. You see, I've never forgotten what you told me the Sunday night before we were married."

Ben stopped abruptly, for he saw the change in his wife's countenance. For a moment, her face was like pale marble. Then anger rushed up as a raging fire and flushed her ashen skin. Her heart was thrown into convulsions, and it was evident in her eyes that this was more than she could bear. Ben's heart was touched by the sight. He knew her anger was not directed at him, but for the horror of the past. He tried to amend the situation.

"Louise, don't feel so badly. You see, Drowd reminded me of it with some of his bragging words the other day. And I love you so much that I couldn't get over it."

Louise had bowed her head and hot tears cascaded down her cheeks, but she uttered no sound. Her heart bled silently from the wound she had just suffered.

Then she announced coldly, "I wish I were dead." She stood and walked toward the bedroom. At the door, she turned and looked tenderly at Ben, who sat shocked and ashamed at what he had done.

"Ben, I wish you could love me for what I am now, instead of hating me for what I was in the past. The year before we were married, I was true to you. And since our wedding, my thoughts have been only of you. God has kept me, Ben. He has made me a new creature, not only for Himself but also for you." She hesitated. "But if this thing has to be always between us, then I'd rather leave today and move as far away as possible, never to hear from anyone in Winston as long as I live."

Ben rose and went to her. He knew he had been wrong and that he must make up to her for this horrible mistake. He pulled Louise into his arms and held her face next to his. Her slender body pressed close to him, and she wept on his shoulder for several minutes.

"Louise, I was wrong. Something tried to tell me that you didn't love me with all your heart, but I know you do." Her hands caressed his face gently, and though she didn't speak, Ben knew he was forgiven.

"Darling, I wish we could erase this past hour from our lives. But I am so thankful that you are willing to forgive me," he whispered.

For a moment, neither spoke. Then Louise lifted her head and looked into his eyes. "Darling, even if you despised me, my love for you is so great that I couldn't hold it against you."

Ben knew she spoke truthfully. He pulled her to him again and covered her warm, sweet lips with his own. The kiss renewed their vows of matrimony, and they embraced a long time.

"I love you, my dearest," Ben whispered, looking into her eyes.

"And I love you, too," replied Louise.

"That makes me happy," said Ben, as Louise turned to go wash her face.

"I guess I should work in the garden for a little while," mused Ben, as he headed toward the bedroom.

"I have put some work clothes out for you," called Louise from the bathroom.

Ben was soon dressed in khaki shorts and tee shirt as he strolled into the kitchen where Louise was clearing the dishes.

"You want to go outside with me, honey?" he asked.

"I'll come out after I clean up, okay?" she responded.

"Sure. I'll work 'til you get there, and then we'll play." He kissed her lips lightly and then went outside.

Ben got a hoe and a garden plow from the storage room, then walked to the little garden behind the house. He loved agriculture, and he and Louise both enjoyed vegetables. He stopped to admire his garden plot, about 20' wide and 40' long. There were a dozen or more rows of fall vegetables. He dropped the hoe and began pushing the plow down one of the furrows.

Thirty minutes later, Louise started toward the garden. She almost called out to Ben, then realized he had not seen her. She walked quietly to the edge of the garden, and stood at the end of the rows, with a teasing smile on her lips. She admired the firmness of Ben's body and his warm tan. His blond hair was already dampened with perspiration. Louise looked at his hands, which firmly grasped the plow handles, and remembered how tenderly and lovingly they always caressed her. Had he not been so engrossed in his work, she would have slipped up close and hugged him hungrily, and coaxed him back into the house . . . . Ben was truly a fine man, and she thanked God every night for having brought the two of them together.

Ben turned and started towards her, pushing vigorously on the plow. A thin layer of dirt slivered silently to the roots of the young vegetables. This was Ben's hobby and he dearly loved it. The smell of the rich soil as he plowed was a delight to his nostrils. About halfway down the row, Louise's voice startled him.

"You look like a real farmer, honey," said Louise, gently laughing at him.

"Girl, don't scare me like that! I'll plow up this whole garden." He stopped and sighed, wiping his damp face on the sleeve of his tee shirt.

"It's looking great," complimented Louise, eyeing the freshly turned furrows.

"Yes, if we can get some rain, we'll have plenty of fresh vegetables," said Ben, as he began to plow again. "Let me finish this row."

"Okay. I'll pull the grass out of this one." She stooped and began to pull the grass and weeds from the earth. They worked diligently for half an hour, and soon only the green leaves of the vegetables showed themselves on the black soil.

"I'm glad we bought this place, instead of that one across town," commented Louise contentedly.

"Yes, I am, too. We couldn't have a garden there, and this is rewarding recreation for me." He stepped closer to his wife. "In fact, I am proud of everything I've got." He looked meaningfully and longingly at Louise from the top of her head to her small feet.

"Are you really, dear?" questioned Louise, turning her sparkling eyes to his.

At that moment, they heard the doorbell.

"I'll see who it is," said Louise, hurrying to the house.

"Okay, sweet. I'll put away the tools and join you." He picked up the hoe and turned to get the plow.

When Ben entered the house, he recognized the pleasant voice of Reverend Paul Jenkins, pastor of the church. He walked into the parlor and greeted the minister heartily.

"Good afternoon, sir. How are you today?" asked Ben.

"Hello, Ben. I am fine. And you?" replied Pastor Jenkins, rising from his chair.

"Oh, I'm fine, but my hands are too dirty for shaking," laughed Ben, exposing his soil-covered hands.

"No problem, Ben," Pastor Jenkins seated himself again.

"I told Brother Jenkins he found us rather untidy," stated Louise as she came from the kitchen, drying her hands.

"I like you working people," teased the pastor, grinning broadly.

"Excuse me, and I'll get washed up," said Ben, as he left the room.

"You should have brought Mrs. Jenkins with you," commented Louise, as she settled onto the couch.

"Well, I was making some calls and decided to stop and ask a favor of you," advised Pastor Jenkins.

"You know I'll do my best for you," reassured Louise.

"You surely are working hard on a Wednesday, Pastor," interrupted Ben, as he returned.

"This is one of my hardest days, Ben. But I do enjoy being busy."

Reverend Jenkins, though middle aged, was a friend to the entire town. He had long ago won the confidence of Ben and Louise.

"Let me state my reason for coming and be on my way, since it's so late," he said, glancing at his watch. "I want you and Sue Martin to sing tonight," he continued, looking at Louise.

"Oh, I would love that! We sang together the other day. She has a lovely soprano voice," responded Louise.

"Yes, one of the best I've heard. And she's a devout Christian and a good church worker, too," responded Pastor Jenkins.

"She surely seems to know a great deal about the Bible. And I heard recently that she's the best nurse at the hospital," contributed Ben.

"Yes, she's an excellent Bible scholar," agreed the pastor enthusiastically. "Well, I must go. I told Miss Martin and Don to be at the church at six-thirty to practice. Can you make that, Louise? It's only a quarter hour from now."

Louise looked at Ben. "I guess we can, can't we, honey?"

"Certainly. Some music would help me. But no need for you to rush, Pastor."

"Yes, I must. I'm expecting the state superintendent to arrive any moment, and he'll be in the service tonight." He hurried out the door and down the steps.

"Thanks for stopping by," called Ben, as he watched Pastor Jenkins get in his blue Celebrity station wagon.

Ben turned to Louise and suggested, "Let's walk to the church."

"Okay. It's always fun walking with you." Louise hurriedly changed her shoes.

As they walked quickly toward the church, Ben teased, "Are you going to fall out before we get there?"

"I never have before. After all, I have to walk by myself quite often when you don't come with me," she reminded Ben, squeezing his hand.

"Maybe you won't have to do that many more times."

"That would make me very, very happy," answered Louise, as they neared the church.

"Don is already here," observed Ben. "I hear his racket."

"Yes, he's never late. And what lovely racket he makes," commented Louise, entering the sanctuary.

Don Drane was the son of Ellis Drane, a superintendent at the pulp mill. He was the best musician in Lincoln County and had played for this church for four years. He also worked in the office at the mill. He was tall and thin, with long slender hands that seemed made for the organ. When he saw the couple, he ceased playing.

"Hello, big shot," called Ben.

"Good evening to you both," responded Don. He rose from the organ bench.

"Oh, don't stop just because we came in," said Louise. "We enjoy your playing."

"He doesn't want to continue in the presence of a superb musician like me," said Ben, pretending an air of superiority.

The three laughed heartily, and Don quipped, "That's right, Ben. Your playing does something to me."

"Yes, and it does something to me, too," teased Louise.

"You two don't have to rub it in," reminded Ben. "Don, how are your new tricks?"

"I don't know any new ones, Ben. I haven't had time to come to you to learn any," answered Don.

It was well known in Winston that Ben Shank was a great comedian. In fact, some folks suggested he should join the circus as a clown. Not that they wanted him to leave town, of course. He and Don often shared their latest antics with each other.

"What are you going to sing tonight?" Don asked Louise.

"I don't know yet. Let's decide when Miss Martin gets here."

"She should be here any minute," said Don as he returned to the organ bench.

Louise sat on the front pew and began thumbing through a hymnal. Ben joined her as though he would help make the selection.

At that moment, the side door opened and slim Sue Martin entered. She wore a plaid skirt, a blue turtleneck, and a light jacket.

"Hello, everyone. I'm sorry I'm late, but I've been rather busy since I got up at 1:30," apologized Sue, approaching the organ.

"Well, you're a minute late, but we'll excuse you this once," smiled Don.

Sue returned his smile. "Please do."

Don had often tried unsuccessfully to get a date with Sue. Indeed, several of the young men in Winston had noticed the attractive nurse, but none had succeeded in taking her out yet. In fact, until a few days ago, Sue's mind had been filled with more important matters. No one knew the secret she and Joe Norton shared -- they figured everyone would find out soon enough without their telling it.

"What shall we sing?" questioned Louise, looking at Sue.

"I haven't thought about it," confessed Sue. "I assumed you would have decided on something." She leafed through the hymnal.

"How does your family like Winston, Sue?" asked Ben.

"We like it fine now. I didn't think I would like to work at this hospital, but I'm enjoying it more and more. And this church helps, too. It means a lot to work and worship in a good church family."

"It certainly does," agreed Louise.

"Why don't you sing 'Whispering Hope'?" asked Ben, looking at the song in the hymnal he held.

"What number is it?" asked Louise.

"One hundred ninety-two. I really like this song," responded Ben.

"It's all right with me," replied Louise, as she turned to it. "Sue, is that okay with you?"

"Oh, yes. It's beautiful, and very appropriate for tonight," agreed Sue, as she stepped nearer to the organ.

"I'm sure you two will make us proud," commented Don, as he began an introduction.

"Will you stand by the organ tonight?" queried Ben.

"I think it would be better to stand behind the pulpit," Sue answered.

"You can practice here and sing there during the service," suggested Don.

Ben looked at the faces of the two young women as they sang. He knew they had become friends in the past few weeks, and he felt they would become as close as sisters in the future. Sue was about an inch taller than Louise. Their features were altogether different, but one was equally as attractive as the other. Of course, Ben found his gaze resting on the face of his beloved Louise, for he had decided long ago that she was the most gorgeous woman he had ever known.

The girls harmonized well. Since Sue had been in town, they had sung together several times. Ben's ears heard the lovely music, but more than that, his heart was touched with the message of the song. A tear found its way down his cheek and he bowed his head, hoping no one would notice.

After the girls finished the song, Don insisted they do it again. Then he switched off the organ and remarked, "There's no need for you ladies to practice any more on that one. It was perfect."

"Thank you, sir," said Louise, as both girls smiled at him.

"Yes, it was marvelous," agreed Ben, rising from the pew.

Louise took his hand. "Thank you, dear. We sang it just for you."

Don locked the organ and looked hopefully at Sue. "Do you have a way home?"

"Yes, I have my dad's car," she replied.

"Too bad. I thought maybe I'd get to drive you home." He smiled wistfully.

"Maybe some other time, Don."

"I'll see you all tonight," called Don, as he walked up the aisle.

"Come to the house with us, Sue," said Louise.

"No, thanks, I still have a few things I must do before the service tonight," declined Sue.

Ben and Louise didn't know that Sue had a very special date and wanted to have herself and the house ready for company.

"Okay, we'll let you off today, but you must come over more often," said Louise in a coaxing tone.

"I'll visit before long. And you two must visit us sometimes," invited Sue, as she got into her father's car. Louise and Ben watched as she drove away.

"Sue is such a fine person, Ben," commented Louise.

"Yes, she seems to be. Let's get home -- it's getting cool out here."

For several minutes neither of them spoke as they walked, then Louise continued, "I wish that Joe and Sue could get together."

"Oh, that guy's too busy to give a girl a second thought," responded Ben.

"Maybe you're right, but they would make such a lovely couple," said Louise. She didn't dream that even now this wish was coming to pass.

They entered their home and Ben closed the door. He pulled Louise close to him and kissed her warmly on the lips. "I'm so proud of you, darling."

"No prouder than I am of you, dear," whispered Louise.

Later she reminded him, "We must hurry and eat a bite before church. What would you like?"

"Oh, I don't know. Let's just fix something together."

In surprise, Louise asked, "You mean you're going to help me?"

"I certainly will. It'll be fun."

As they busied themselves in the cozy kitchen, their laughter and gay chatter would have made one think they were playing house.

Sue helped her mother spruce up the living room. All the Martins were looking forward to Joe's arrival. Sue's sister, Sharon, had talked of nothing else since she got home from school at three-thirty. She was twelve years old, and she and Sue were close friends.

The Martin home was just ordinary, but neat and tidy. Mrs. Martin had started improving the yard and would beautify it more when spring came.

"Everything looks okay to me," said Sue, as she sat down and glanced around the room.

"Of course it is. He probably won't even look around, anyway. Men don't notice things the way women do," advised Mrs. Martin.

Sue laughed. "The way we're behaving, you'd think this date was some grand occasion."

"When is Daddy coming home, Mother?" asked Sharon.

"I'm not sure. He called and said he has to work overtime."

Sue frowned. "Daddy has worked so hard since we moved here."

"Yes, the superintendent who preceded him at the mill left it in a mess. However, he's put together an excellent work force, and almost all the machines are operational again. Maybe things will be better when we get adjusted to our new work environments," said Mrs. Martin. "I must start supper, since Joe is not taking all of us to eat."

"What are we eating tonight, Mother?" asked Sharon.

"I think I'll make an Irish stew," replied Mrs. Martin thoughtfully.

Sue stood. "I guess I'll get ready. Joe will be here soon."

"Dear, you're not very enthusiastic about this date, are you?" asked her mother gently.

"Well, Mother, you know I have dedicated my life to God. I don't want to do anything that will hinder me in my spiritual relationship with Him. Even though Joe is a good man, he is not a Christian." She hesitated, then plunged ahead. "But I feel it will be all right to date him. His family members are Christians, and I intend to try to win him to Christ."

"Well, this may be a splendid opportunity for you. But no matter what happens, don't slack up in your Christian walk," cautioned Mrs. Martin.

"Oh, don't you worry. God has been too real and wonderful for me to turn from Him," promised Sue, as she headed toward her room.

Mr. Martin arrived home and Mrs. Martin told him Joe would be there soon. He and Sharon were laughing and talking when Sue entered the living room.

"My, you surely are dolled up for this young man," commented Mr. Martin.

Sue was dressed in an emerald green suit with gold buttons. The outfit was a perfect backdrop for her blond hair as it shimmered on her shoulders. "Hello, Dad. I hope you didn't have a hard day." She looked at her watch as she sat next to him on the couch.

"No, not too bad. But Mother won't give me anything to eat until this Romeo of yours has come and gone. And I'm starved!" He delighted in teasing his daughters.

Sharon, who was by the window, saw a car turn into the driveway and advised, "This must be Joe now. Daddy, you behave yourself."

As Sue opened the door, Joe was getting out of his car. She was aware of the thrill that ran through her being. As he walked toward the house, Joe experienced an equal sensation as he heard Sue say, "Come in, Joe. It's nice to see you again."

"Hello, Sue. I'm a bit early because my sister and my dad teased me so much that I left as soon as I was dressed."

"We have something in common then," replied Sue, and they both chuckled.

When the door was closed behind him, Joe turned to meet the Martins. Mr. Martin and Sharon were on the couch, and Mrs. Martin stood in the doorway that led to the kitchen.

"Joe Norton, this is my mother, my father, and my sister Sharon," stated Sue.

"Hello. It's a pleasure to meet you all," responded Joe. All three of the Martins nodded and spoke in unison, "Hello."

"We're glad to have you with us, Joe," said Mr. Martin. "Sit down."

"Thank you, sir." He slipped into the nearest chair. He was a striking young man. He wore brown trousers and a light tan sport coat, with a brown lapel handkerchief. His eyes were especially bright with excitement this evening.

"They have you all working long hours at the mill, don't they?" asked Joe of Mr. Martin.

"Yes, we're rather busy," replied Mr. Martin.

"Well, if we are going to make it to church on time, we'd better go," said Sue.

"Yes, we should go. Though I wish I had time to pick at Sharon a little," responded Joe, as he stood. Sharon's cheeks flushed pink, but she smiled sweetly.

"We wish you didn't have to rush, but we do want you to be at church," agreed Mrs. Martin.

"Oh, we'll be there," Joe assured her.

Sue pulled a light wrap around her shoulders and indicated to Joe with a smile that she was ready.

"I'm glad to have met you all," Joe stated, somewhat nervously.

Mr. Martin rose from the couch. "Thank you, Joe. And you come back."

"Yes, do come again," added Mrs. Martin.

"Thank you. We'll see you at church in a little while. Bye-bye, bashful Sharon," said Joe.

They all laughed and turned to look at Sharon. There was a look of friendship in her eyes.

"Be careful and sweet," cautioned Mrs. Martin.

"Okay, Mother," replied Sue, as the door closed behind them.

Joe opened the car door for Sue and she slipped onto the seats of his Oldsmobile. Sue noticed again that the interior still smelled of new leather. Soon they were driving toward town.

"Is there a particular place you'd like to eat, Sue?" questioned Joe.

"No. I've not eaten out much in Winston, so I don't know the restaurants. Anywhere that is nice will suit me."

"The Ranche is about fifteen miles out of Winston on Highway 28. I thought we might go there," said Joe, as he stopped at a traffic light.

Sue responded, "That's fine with me."

After the light changed, Joe continued down Main Street. "There's the church. It's been a while since I was there, but I'm glad I'm going tonight."

"I hope you become a regular attendee, Joe," said Sue seriously.

"I don't think it will require much encouragement on the part of a certain girl I know to keep me going," replied Joe, stealing a glance at her.

Sue laughed softly. They rode in silence for a couple of miles. Though they were nervous, each of them secretly hoped this was the beginning of a long friendship. Sue had a great desire to win Joe to an active faith in Christ. And he was the first young man she had been interested enough in to date since her folks had moved to Winston.

"How's your work at the hospital?" queried Joe.

"Fine. At first, I didn't think I would like it, because I was at a much larger hospital before. But now I like the smaller one better," Sue replied.

"From now on, every time I get a headache, I'm going to the hospital for treatment," teased Joe.

"Great. I like to take care of good patients."

"Dr. Blair is a friend of mine, and he's also our family doctor," advised Joe.

"He's about the best doctor here, I think. Your sister had told me he was your family doctor. I work with him quite often."

"Oh, I had forgotten that you've already met my sister Ann."

"Yes, and I like her. We have become friends. And your mother is sweet, too. It seems the people of Winston have a real respect for her," confided Sue.

"Sis is a good girl, and of course, Mother has always been wonderful to me," agreed Joe.

"I haven't been around your dad enough to form an opinion, but he seems to be a hard-working man," continued Sue.

"He's okay. I'm a lot like him -- except for the hard work," laughed Joe.

Sue chuckled, but countered, "Well, from what I've learned, there is some of that in you, too."

"Here we are at The Ranche, and I'm hungry," stated Joe. He pulled up in front of a large, well-lighted building.

After Joe opened her door, they walked toward the restaurant. A couple sat in a car nearby, and they greeted Joe. "They're from Winston," Joe informed Sue.

They entered a beautiful dining room. Tables were in the front of the room and booths were in the back area. All were covered with white tablecloths. Each table or booth had a small crystal vase with a live rosebud in it. Brass lanterns hung at intervals on the dark wooden walls between hanging baskets of green ferns. The hardwood floors glistened in the soft light. It was one of the loveliest places Sue had ever eaten. She was glad Joe had brought her here.

His voice snapped her out of her reverie. "Do you prefer a table or booth?"

"It doesn't matter to me," she answered dreamily.

"Let's ask for the booth in the back. Then we can talk freely without interruption," suggested Joe.

After the waitress seated them, Sue remarked, "This is one of the most exquisite restaurants I have visited."

"So it looks a little better than the hospital?" asked Joe.

"Oh, yes! I like the hospital, but you must admit, this is quite different."

After they ordered steaks, Sue slipped out of her wrap. Joe politely hung it on the nearby coat tree.

"Thank you, sir," Sue said softly, as he returned to his seat.

"You're very welcome. I'll be glad when those steaks get here. I'm a little hungry, aren't you?"

"Yes, I am. Joe, how far is the lake where you and Mr. Owen fished this afternoon?" she asked.

"It's about fifteen miles north of Winston. Maybe I can take you there soon. It's truly a beautiful lake." Joe reached for the tomato juice the waitress had set before him.

"I've never been boat riding, but I've always wanted to go," Sue said wistfully.

"I'm sure that can be arranged," he responded eagerly.

The steaks arrived, and Sue looked across the table at Joe, who had picked up his fork. He placed it back on the table and looked apologetically into her blue eyes, "Oh, you always give thanks to God before you eat."

"You are very thoughtful," murmured Sue. She bowed her head and prayed a simple prayer of thanksgiving for God's love and the provisions of life. Joe bowed his head, just as he did at home.

"I do admire your consecrated life, Sue -- the way you stand firm for what you believe." He began to cut his steak.

"The Lord has done so much for me, Joe, that I can't forget Him in anything," Sue answered humbly as she started eating. "This is delicious food."

"Ben first brought me here, and he knows the owner well."

"He knows almost everyone around here, doesn't he?" asked Sue.

"Yes, he was in the Army with the owner's son. That's the owner's wife at the register, but I don't see him."

About halfway through the meal, Sue looked up as a well-dressed man entered the restaurant. "Who is that gentleman?"

Joe turned and saw the black hair and sharp face of Jack Drowd. He sighed in disgust and replied, "That's no gentleman -- that's Jack Drowd."

Sue could sense that Joe did not want to discuss this man. It seemed strange that such a fine person as Joe Norton could dislike anyone so intensely as he apparently detested Jack Drowd.

As Sue wondered what was between this man Drowd and her new friend, Joe ate in silence. However, as all that Shep had told him this afternoon came back to him, his food was no longer appetizing. He thought of the young couple he loved so dearly. He shuddered as he imagined Louise in the arms of this maniac. Then he considered what poor Ben must go through every time he saw or thought of Jack Drowd. For the first time in his life, Joe hated. He had never wanted to hate anyone, because he respected his parents' teachings. He tried now to still the storm inside his breast, but it refused to die.

Drowd sat at a small table, placed his order, and looked haughtily around the restaurant. He was always searching for trouble, and when he saw Joe and Sue, he felt this was a good place to start. He strolled casually to their booth.

Joe didn't look up from his plate, but he was aware of Drowd's approach. His nerves tensed and a desire to kill Drowd rose up in him. Even if he had to pay for such a crime, it would free Ben and Louise from their nightmare.

Drowd's keen voice spoke. "Hello, miss. It's most unusual to see a lady with this fellow." His voice dripped with sarcasm.

"Hello." Sue had decided the offense lay in Drowd and not in Joe Norton.

"Hello, Mr. Norton. Why not introduce me to the lady?" sneered Drowd.

Joe lifted his head and Sue gasped in amazement at what she saw. His eyes were like two fiery coals set in chiseled marble. His lips were drawn tight, forming a straight line. When he spoke, it was like a steel whip lashing out cruelly.

"She's not interested in meeting you, Drowd. You've ruined enough folks around here, so shove off. You are not welcome where I am."

"Oh, the big shot Norton is so jealous of Drowd that he doesn't want him around. Now, Joe, you know that Jack Drowd goes with all the girls in Winston," drawled Drowd.

Joe was infuriated beyond control. His heart burned with hatred. His muscles tensed and his right fist clenched as he growled, "Get out of here, before I throw you out, you jailbird."

The color drained from Drowd's face as he, too, became angry. It greatly annoyed him for anyone to refer to his past life -- especially the years he had spent in prison. "If you think you can throw me out, start whenever you're ready," he snarled.

Although Joe had been in very few fights, he was physically strong and powerful. He was known as the best athlete Winston High had ever produced. His daring courage and reckless plays had won them many games. He was not afraid as he faced this man who was skilled in fighting. Joe also knew that Drowd fought dirty and was an excellent knife wielder, but he felt no fear. He started to get up from the booth when a soft voice spoke, as from a great distance. He realized it was Sue.

"Please, Joe," was all she said, but her voice carried such a tender message that Joe's muscles relaxed. The fire left his being and the color returned to his face. His eyes met Sue's, and he was touched when he realized she was holding back tears.

"I'm sorry, Sue," he whispered.

He turned to Drowd and spoke firmly, "I regret that I shall have to pass up this opportunity, Drowd. However, I'm sure the future will provide another."

"Don't you worry. There will be another time," growled Drowd, as he turned away. He hadn't wanted to fight Joe, but he couldn't forget how Shep Owen, Joe's godfather, had smashed a huge fist in his face just days ago.

Joe sat silently, ashamed for what he had said and done in Sue's presence.

"It's getting late, Joe. We should start for the church." She spoke as though nothing unusual had occurred.

Joe signaled for the waitress to bring the check and soon they were on their way. They rode in silence for two miles before Joe spoke.

"Sue, I guess you can never forgive me for what happened and how I behaved."

She moved a little closer to him and said, "Don't worry. I'm sure you had a valid reason. I'm just sorry it spoiled the good time we were having, but I can't hold it against you. I would like an explanation, though."

"I can't tell you now, Sue. But if things work out, then some day I'll explain it and you will understand. I will prove to you that I was doing the right thing tonight," promised Joe.

"All right," replied Sue. She remained quiet for several minutes. She spoke again. "I believe in you, Joe."

Joe stole a glance at her. "Thanks, Sue. I'll prove that I appreciate your trust and confidence just as soon as possible."

They had passed the large "Welcome to Winston" sign. "Well, here we are, back in Winston. We might have been better off to have grabbed a hamburger at Suzie's," laughed Joe.

Sue smiled at him. "I'll never forget the first meal I ate there. I enjoyed it. You know, this is such a peaceful town."

"Yes, considering the terror in the world, it is peaceful. But even Winston gets rough sometimes," commented Joe, as he pulled up in front of the church.

"There's only one place where we can find perfect peace, and that is in Christ," stated Sue.

Joe turned and looked into her lovely face. His heart yearned for her, and his arms longed to pull her close. His lips desired to press those ruby lips which spoke in such a comforting tone. For a few seconds, he allowed himself to dream. Then he said, "Yes, I'm beginning to believe that. We'd better go in -- it's 7:30."

They walked briskly toward the door.

"Looks like a big crowd tonight," remarked Sue.

"Yes, and I see my folks are here. That's Dad's car." He pointed to a green Pontiac parked across the street.

"They are always here," said Sue, "and I hope the other member of the Norton family will become a regular."

"I suspect he won't miss often."

As they entered the vestibule, Sue stated, "The choir is singing."

Shep Owen was one of the ushers. He greeted them. "Hello, boy! I'm glad to see you here. Good evening, Miss Martin."

Sue returned his warm smile, "Hello, Mr. Owen."

"It's good to be here, Shep. This is the secret I wouldn't tell you this afternoon," said Joe.

"Well, it's a pleasant surprise. Where would you two like to sit?" He scanned the auditorium, which was almost packed to capacity.

"I see a place way down there, Shep. Does that suit you, Sue?"

"It's okay," nodded Sue, and started down the aisle.

"I'll see you after the service, Shep," whispered Joe. Then he followed Sue.

They slipped into the vacant spot, then looked up to see Jeff Shawn, a salesman at Winston Hardware, directing the choir in the opening number. Pastor

Jenkins sat in one pulpit chair and the superintendent sat in the other. Don Drane played the organ and Ann Norton the piano. Sue let her gaze rest on Ann for several moments. Ann was so admired by the young men, as well as by the older folks. She was as popular as Joe, and her kind, courteous manners had won her many friends. She and Ann had been friends for several weeks, but now that Sue had met her brother Joe, she looked at Ann in a different light.

Sue caught her wandering thoughts and breathed a prayer that Joe would soon become a Christian and a willing church worker.

The choir ended the first song, and started another. Sue took a hymnal and found the page. Joe reached to hold one edge of the book. Sue was determined this new acquaintance would not hinder her worship, so she began to sing with the choir. Joe listened, then joined in with his bass voice. He had sung in school and Ann had taught him quite a bit about music. Though his voice could not compare with Sue's, he held his own.

After the choir was seated, Pastor Jenkins welcomed everyone and named several ministers who were present. He made various announcements, including the fact that this was a special night for evangelism and an offering would be received. As the ushers came forward, he announced the number of the next hymn. Then he added, "After this song, Mrs. Ben Shank and Miss Martin will sing for us."

Everyone was invited to stand and sing with the choir. Joe moved closer to Sue and asked, "Is that 'Miss Martin' you?"

"I think it is." Sue smiled at him gently.

When Shep Owen passed by with the collection plate, Joe dropped a bill in and Shep slapped him on the back. The song ended, and the choir marched down as the musicians continued to play. Sue slipped quietly out of the pew and down the aisle to the front of the church. Joe watched her go, and felt his heart pounding. He wanted her to be perfect, yet he was afraid she might make a mistake. She reached the platform just as Louise did. Don began playing on the organ, accompanied by Ann at the piano. The two girls began to sing "Whispering Hope." As their voices blended sweetly, Joe's fear left. He realized that Sue would not fail as long as her faith was absolutely in God. As the song continued, he realized also that, though he had everything in life that the natural man would desire, something was lacking. He tried to make himself believe that his need was to be married, to establish a home, and settle down. But in his heart he knew that only a faith in God such as his family possessed would fill the vacancy. A tear slipped silently down his cheek. It was the first tear Joe had ever shed in church, but he was not ashamed.

Sue had been very uneasy while she was singing. She had sung before this congregation and many others, but tonight she wanted to drive home the message of salvation. As she came to her seat, she looked into Joe's face. His eyes met hers, and she noticed the sign of the tear. Her heart was glad because she knew the purpose of the singing had been accomplished. She breathed a silent prayer of thanksgiving to God.

Pastor Jenkins introduced the superintendent, the Reverend M. E. Benis, and left the platform. Reverend Benis preached a stirring message on "Guarding Our Heritage." Afterwards, there was a prayer, and the service was over. A warm atmosphere of fellowship pervaded the sanctuary. Many people spoke to Sue and

Joe. They assured Joe they were delighted to see him in church and invited him to return.

In fifteen minutes, almost everyone was out of the auditorium. Ben and Louise stood talking to Sue and Joe. Ben had made some funny remark, and all were laughing as Pastor Jenkins and Reverend Benis approached.

"Hello," said Pastor Jenkins.

"Hello," four happy voices replied.

"I'd like you to meet Brother Benis. This is Mr. and Mrs. Ben Shank, Joe Norton, and Miss Sue Martin."

"I'm glad to meet you all. I must say, I enjoyed the song you two ladies sang." His voice was quite dignified, as he shook hands with each of them.

"These two young men are the owner, manager, and entire staff of Norton's Motor Parts, Brother Benis," advised Pastor Jenkins.

Amid the laughter, Ben chimed, "Joe is the owner 'flunky' and I'm the rest of that." The six of them chuckled.

"Well, we'll run along, as we have much business to discuss tonight. Joe, we want you to come often," said Pastor Jenkins, as they left the group.

"Come by the house and we'll have a cup of coffee. Maybe Louise would even fix us a snack," invited Ben.

"We don't have time," said Joe. "This lady must change clothes and be at work at ten, and it's already nine."

"I didn't realize it was that late. We need to be going," advised Sue.

"Well, we'll make it another night," stated Louise. "Let's go, too, honey. Five-thirty will come early, and Boss Norton won't like it if you are late."

"Oh? Does he ever get there on time?" laughed Joe pleasantly.

As Ben and Louise walked away, she commented, "Well, there's the couple we had wished to get together. Wonder how they met?"

"I don't know, but they do look nice together," agreed Ben.

After waving to Ben and Louise, Sue turned to Joe. "It looks like we're the last to leave."

"Yes, but let's speak to Mrs. Owen before we go. It will only take a minute."

They walked down the aisle to her wheelchair. Shep always remained to turn off the lights and close the church. He was about ready to carry Mrs. Owen to the car.

"Hello, Mrs. Owen," greeted Sue, extending her hand.

"Hello, dear. I'm glad to see you. I must say that song did me so much good." She grasped Sue's hand warmly.

"Hello, young lady," said Joe, taking her other hand.

"Hello, son. You'll never know the blessing I received when I looked back and saw you in the congregation tonight."

"I enjoyed the service and I'll be coming back," Joe informed her.

"It is my prayer that you'll attend regularly and be a great worker here in the near future, Joe."

"Did Shep try to convince you that he caught the biggest fish this afternoon?" asked Joe, as Shep approached them.

"Oh, yes. He always catches the biggest. I'm sure you two had a swell time today."

"Boy, it is great to see you in church," said Shep.

"I'm happy to be here. You have all invited me so many times, but it took only one invitation from the right person." He looked starrily at Sue, who blushed. She was not just proud to have brought a visitor to church. She was truly glad to have met such a kind and considerate young businessman in the midst of such a crooked world.

"We'd better run along. Sue has to be at the hospital by ten."

"Yes, and they won't let me work in this outfit," smiled Sue.

"We have to go, too," said Shep.

"Good night to you both," called Mrs. Owen, as they departed.

Sue was acutely aware of how happy she was as they walked down the steps toward the car. She felt as though she had known Joe Norton a long time. Neither spoke until they were in the car.

"I am glad I came," Joe stated, as he drove down Main Street.

"Did you really enjoy it?" Sue asked.

"Yes, especially that song. I didn't know you could sing so beautifully."

"Oh, I can't," Sue said humbly, "but I do love to try."

"It's good enough for me. I want to hear more of it."

Sue asked, "Didn't I hear you singing with the congregation?"

"Oh, I sing a little. Ann has tried to teach me about music," Joe confided.

"There's Norton's Motor Parts!" exclaimed Sue.

"Yes, I'd almost forgotten it," admitted Joe. "You know, going to church makes you forget your problems and worries."

"That's what I've tried to tell you this week, Joe," responded Sue softly.

"Well, you've convinced me, and I'll be going back. Of course, I like good company when I go," smiled Joe.

"Yes, I even enjoyed the service better tonight," confessed Sue.

Joe pulled up in front of the bungalow where Sue's folks lived and they got out of the car. "Your mother surely keeps things nice. This yard is about the neatest one around here," he complimented.

"Mother loves a clean house and yard and plenty of flowers."

As they entered the house, Sharon greeted them. "I thought you two had forgotten all about work tonight," she laughed gaily.

"We almost did," said Joe as he closed the door.

"Sit down, Joe, while I change to my uniform. It's only twenty minutes until I must check in."

Mr. Martin invited, "Yes, Joe, have a seat. I was eating the dessert that I didn't have time for before church."

Joe made himself comfortable in a nearby chair.

"Would you like some pie while you wait?" asked Mrs. Martin from the kitchen doorway.

"No, thank you, Mrs. Martin," Joe declined.

"It's getting cool outside," continued Sue's father.

"Yes, sir. It will probably freeze soon. I guess it's time we had a little cold weather." Joe was thinking how pleasant Sue's family was.

"My, I hope it doesn't get too cold," worried Mrs. Martin.

"Oh, I hope it snows about six inches," chimed Sharon.

"What do you think you are -- a snowbird?" teased her father.

Sue entered the room hurriedly. "I hate to rush, Joe, but we really must go."

"I'm ready when you are, Miss Martin," he said gallantly.

"I thought maybe you could take the car, Sue, and Joe could stay and talk with us," interrupted Sharon.

Sue colored slightly. "Sharon, you always say the wrong thing." Mr. and Mrs. Martin laughed, and Joe joined in when he realized this was their way of showing affection.

"I'm glad to have met you all and hope to see you again soon," said Joe.

"Thanks, Joe. You come back," invited Mr. Martin.

"Sue, shall I pick you up from work tomorrow morning?" asked her mother.

"No, thanks. I'll get a taxi home," advised Sue, as she kissed Mrs. Martin.

"Good night, you big tease," Joe told Sharon.

Sharon responded. "Good night. Don't get lost on the way to the hospital."

The door closed behind them.

"You look wonderful in your 'working clothes'," said Joe, as he started the car.

"Thank you. This is what they say all good nurses must wear."

Joe drove quickly to the hospital. "Here we are, nurse."

"Joe, we have a rule that dates may not come in, so I'll say good night here."

"I understand. Say, may I be that taxi that takes you home tomorrow morning?"

She considered. "Joe, I get off at six-thirty and that's quite early."

"No problem. I get up at five-thirty, and it would be my pleasure."

She looked steadily into his brown eyes. "Okay, if you want. I have truly enjoyed the evening, Joe."

"So have I," he answered.

Their eyes held a moment, leaving Sue breathless. She felt Joe take her hand in his. At first, she wanted to pull her hand away, but she yielded and then gradually responded with equal pressure. It was a simple, thrilling moment. Neither said a word but their feelings told them many exciting things.

Sue loosed her hand. "I'd better go."

"I'll see you in the morning, Miss Martin," Joe spoke softly.

Just before she closed the door, she looked back at him and said, "Okay, Mr. Businessman."

She watched Joe drive away, then ran up the steps and into the hospital. Her heart was singing. She knew now that Joe was more than a casual friend. As she worked her shift that night, she kept remembering the soft squeeze of Joe's hand on hers.

The full moon glided noiselessly through the inky sky just above the treetops. It seemed all its rays were reflected in the waters of the placid lake of Little River State Park. One could easily imagine that the moon kept a secret. The stars glimmered in the vault of the heavens like millions of rhinestones. The park was blanketed in silence except for the water spilling over the dam and racing toward the rocks below. Occasionally, a lonely katydid added its music to the setting. The December night was crystal clear. Though it was chilly, the young couple who sat in the Oldsmobile overlooking the lake did not notice. They were enamored with each other and the breathtaking display of God's handiwork before them.

"Sue, I have grown very fond of you," Joe spoke softly.

Sue looked briefly at Joe's face, then back to the lake. "I could say the same to you, Joe, but I'm afraid it isn't for the best."

Her words stunned him. How could she not reciprocate these feelings that had become so intense over these past few months? They had been together every night for the past month. Sue did not have to work tonight, so they had decided to visit the park.

"What do you mean, Sue?" Joe asked in bewilderment.

"It's hard to explain. Since I met you at Suzie's, I have admired you, Joe. I will never forget our first date. When you left me at the hospital that night, I knew then that I loved you." She hesitated, noticing that Joe was breathing hard and had a stricken look on his face. "I have tried to control my love for you, but it has steadily grown. And I have longed for this time to come, but I have been afraid to face it. Only God can understand my feelings."

"But, Sue, I feel the same about you. I've spent hours at night planning our future together. The greatest desire of my heart is to make you my wife -- to build you a home and to make you happy."

He reached for Sue's hand, but she took it away. Joe had never tried to kiss Sue because of his great respect for her. But they had often held hands. This was the first time she had refused. He looked at the lovely face turned earnestly toward him in the moonlight. He saw compassion in her blue eyes and a trace of sadness. He couldn't bear the possibility that the dreams and air castles he had been building were about to crumble.

"Joe, I hope we can understand each other."

"Sue, the only thing I understand is that if I am robbed of you, then I'd rather be at the bottom of that lake," Joe admitted hoarsely.

"Don't say that. I told you my love for you is as great as yours for me. But let me explain."

Sue bowed her head and sat silently for a few minutes. Joe longed to stroke the blond hair so close to his shoulder, but he dared not. When she lifted her head, he saw through the moonlight the tears streaming down her cheeks. She spoke in a low, hollow tone, firmly and from her heart.

"Joe, you know I have dedicated my life to God. Four years ago, I started training as a nurse for Him. For a long time, He has dealt with me about going to South America as a missionary. That's why I've made such rapid progress in nursing -- because God has helped me. I've never had time for anything else but to fulfill the call of God in my life until I met you. But I must go on and do His perfect will. Do you understand, Joe?"

He didn't speak for a moment. The moon no longer looked beautiful nor the stars joyful. The water was like a beast waiting for its prey. It appeared the hand of God had been withdrawn from the park and the powers of hell had moved in. Joe knew the devil was the author of confusion, and it seemed his talons had clutched the park scene. He turned to Sue.

"I have been taught to honor and respect God and His work, Sue. I can't say anything against that. But I have also been taught that God is love. Surely if we love each other, He will not separate us."

"Joe, try to understand. If I could have my way, then I would be yours and yours alone. But my love for God and His work is greater than anything else in my life. I must do His will."

Joe did believe that Sue loved him. And he truly didn't want to come between her and God, even though he knew he was not a Christian. "Sue, let's forget the serious part of this and be friends. I am sure God will work things out for the best. Much better than we can." This was the only response Joe could manage. He was near tears, but too proud to allow her to see his pain.

"Joe, I only wish you were a Christian so you could help me pray about this," her voice was as sweet and sincere as ever.

Joe replied, "I know I need to be, Sue. But I *have* started attending church regularly."

"Everyone needs to be saved, Joe, but don't wait until it is too late. You know mankind doesn't have too much time," reminded Sue.

The words "too late" pierced his heart like a dagger. He had been too late a few times in the business world and had missed some excellent deals. He knew he must not be too late in his acceptance of Christ, because the only place to get right was in this life. Yet he could not bring himself to make that commitment yet. But he wanted to placate Sue in some way and prevent her from slipping through his fingers. "I promise I would go to church with you, Sue. And I would never try to come between you and God. Please keep praying for me."

She glanced at her watch. "It's eleven-thirty, Joe. We have to get up early tomorrow."

"Yes. Your mom will be on my case if I keep you out past twelve."

As he started the car, Sue asked, "Have you forgotten that tomorrow is Christmas Eve?"

"No. Ann is supposed to use my car. But we still have a date for tomorrow night, don't we?"

"I didn't break it, so I'll be waiting for you. Ann must be planning a big day."

Joe replied, "She and some of the girls are going to decorate the church for the Christmas program. She won't tell me much about it."

"God is using her in a wonderful way," said Sue.

"Ann has been a ray of sunshine in our home since Mother got sick. Dad is always busy and worries about Mother, too. I've been trying to get my business off the ground. I guess we couldn't get along without Ann."

"I know they will have the church decorated beautifully tomorrow night."

"Oh, Ann likes decorating," agreed Joe. "By the way, did I tell you that Dad and I are giving her a car for Christmas?"

"Oh, my goodness! I know she'll be happy. Is it a new car?" asked Sue.

"Yes. A red Honda Accord. Shep will deliver it Christmas morning. She thinks I'm buying her a coat. She's accused Dad of not getting her anything." Joe chuckled.

"I don't know anyone who will appreciate it more than Ann," commented Sue.

"Well, here's your place. Looks like your folks are in bed." He turned into the Martins' drive.

"Yes. They are planning a big day tomorrow. Dad is off, so it's a shame I have to work. But I will be off Christmas Day."

"So will I," said Joe, as he opened the door of the car for her. When they reached the steps, Sue stepped onto the first one, bringing her to Joe's eye level.

"Joe, I'm glad tonight is over. I'm not afraid any longer, because I know God will work out our lives so that we will be happy."

"I'm sure He will." He reached for Sue's hand and held it firmly. "No matter what happens Sue, I love you, and I always will."

Sue hesitated, then spoke gently, "I feel the same, Joe. You'd better go now. I'll see you tomorrow night."

He lifted her hand and pressed it against his lips tenderly.

"Good night, dearest," she whispered, as he turned toward the car.

Joe drove straight home, parked the car, and walked toward the house. There was a light in the den, and he wondered who was up at this hour. Rags, Ann's big collie dog, came to meet him. He patted him on the head and said, "I guess you and Mother would wait up for me no matter how late I came home."

Rags wagged his tail and nuzzled Joe's hand, as if he understood perfectly. The Norton family had a faithful friend in this dog.

Joe looked into the sky and saw the dark clouds from the northeast partially covering the moon. It was growing colder and darker, and occasionally, a flash of lightning illuminated the countryside, revealing the young man gazing heavenward with his hand on the dog's head.

To Joe, the clouds symbolized the sorrow he had just experienced. He had put on a bold front with Sue, but it was the blackest moment his heart had ever known. As he stood trying to make sense of it all, the clouds parted momentarily and the moon was visible. He could see Sue's lovely face, the big blue eyes that had been mystic pools of sympathy and compassion for all her friends. He saw the blond hair that reached her shoulders. More than anything, Joe wanted to make Sue his own. He wanted to hold her close to himself forever. Then the wind pushed another black cloud over the moon, and his reverie was broken. Rags moved closer, and he remembered that he was home and it was very cold. He patted the dog's head again and walked wearily into the house.

Inside Ann was decorating pine cones with clusters of holly, ribbon, and glitter. "Come in, mister. I have to get all these decorated and get some sleep before we start working at the church at seven o'clock in the morning. Don't you want a job?" She lifted a tired face from where she sat between two boxes of cones, one box decorated and the other waiting to be.

Joe removed his coat and began to work with his sister. "My, you girls are getting an early start."

"We have to, Joe. It will take most of the day to get the church ready. Then we have the last rehearsal at 4:30." Ann wearily pushed a lock of hair back and yawned.

"Sounds like Christmas Eve won't be much pleasure for you," Joe remarked.

"I'll be lucky if I live through it," replied Ann.

"Well, you'd better, or some of us had just as soon be dead."

"Oh, I doubt I would be missed until they called the roll at school," laughed Ann.

"Let's not talk like that -- it's too serious," stated Joe. A heavy silence followed that both felt intensely, yet neither understood. An ominous foreboding seemed to have settled like a blanket over the room. Joe tried to shake off the depressive atmosphere.

"Why don't you go on to bed and get some rest, Ann? I'll finish these."

"No, it will take only a few more minutes," she said.

"I know one person around here who is certainly asleep," commented Joe, nodding toward their parents' bedroom.

"Yes, Dad has been snoring for a couple of hours," advised Ann.

"What time did Mother go to bed?" asked Joe.

"About ten. She wanted to stay up until you came in, but I insisted she go to bed. She worked extra hard today and needed the rest."

"Bless her heart. You know, she would do anything for either of us," Joe said tenderly.

"And I'll tell you something else, Joe," began Ann. "Mother and Dad are both happy that you have started going to church with Sue."

"I'm glad to hear that. I've done a lot to make Mother worry. Maybe now I can help make her happy."

"Her only real worry is that you become a Christian. She has told me many times that she prays God will let her see you accept Christ before she dies." Ann spoke seriously.

"Well, I *am* going to church," Joe said, a little testily.

"I think God may be working through Sue Martin to bring you to Himself," stated Ann.

She didn't see the change in his countenance. He felt a sharp sting of pain in his heart, and a shadow crossed his face. He didn't reply.

Ann reached for the last cone, but Joe beat her to it. "I'll do it. You get to bed."

"Okay. Joe, I'm very proud of my big brother, and I want you to be happy." As she passed him, she placed a hand gently on his shoulder. "I'll see you at five-thirty."

"Okay, Sis. And the feeling is mutual. No man could be prouder of his little sister than I am of you."

After Ann left the room, Joe's eyes filled with tears as he thought about Ann. They had always been very close, but tonight had seemed special in some indefinable way. He looked at Ann's picture on the desk. "Oh, what would I do without her?"

Joe's mind was filled with such confusion that he could not sleep when he lay down. He knew Christmas

Eve would be the busiest day of the year at Norton's Motor Parts, but he could only roll and toss. Sue's blue eyes haunted him all night. He wished he had never seen her. Then he knew his life would have been incomplete without her. When he heard his dad arise at five o'clock, he decided he could not solve this dilemma. "I'm just a guy in love, I guess. Might as well get busy."

When he entered the kitchen, Mr. Norton was pouring himself a cup of coffee. He grinned at the sight of Joe and commented, "Good morning, boy. You look like you've been up for at least a week."

"I feel like I've been up a month. Pour me a cup of that black magic," requested Joe, as he sat at the table.

"I don't know if you can handle it this strong," teased his dad. He placed a cup in front of Joe. He and his son seemed more like brothers than father and son.

"Well, I see you've drunk half a pot and it hasn't killed you."

"Why didn't you sleep last night, son? Were you excited about the big day at the store?" asked Mr. Norton.

"Oh, I don't know. That may be part of it."

"My, my. Probably won't sell ten dollars worth," teased his father.

"At least, I won't have to mend fences and run cows." Joe had never liked farm work. Though his dad sometimes accused him of being lazy, that didn't bother Joe. He had proved to everyone in Winston that he was a businessman.

"Why don't you two stop this racket, so someone else can sleep?" asked Ann, as she entered, rubbing her eyes.

"Well, here's another one who stayed up all night," grinned Mr. Norton.

"Not quite, but I feel like I did," she replied, pouring herself a cup of coffee. "Mother's getting up now."

"Hope she's going to cook some breakfast," murmured Joe.

"What's the matter, big boy? Couldn't you eat my cooking?" asked Ann.

"Well, if you feel like you look, it wouldn't be fit to eat," grinned Joe.

As they all laughed, Mrs. Norton came in and said, "You Nortons are the biggest teasers in the world."

She continued, "Good morning, son. Hope you're ready for a big day."

"Hello, Mother."

"Say, are you in the Christmas spirit?" Mr. Norton asked his wife as she began to prepare breakfast.

"Yes, I am. I feel better than I have for a long time. And, by the way, what have you got me for Christmas?"

"And what do you have for me, Dad?" chimed Ann.

"To tell you the truth, darling, I don't have you anything yet. But if I can get what I have in mind, you'll be the most popular girl in Winston," he smiled happily at Ann.

At six o'clock, breakfast was over and the family had their usual devotion. Ann read the account of Mary and Joseph just prior to the birth of Christ. After the prayer, she suggested to Joe that he should read the rest of the story tomorrow morning.

Joe and Mr. Norton loaded Ann's decorations for the church into Joe's car, and the two young people were ready to go.

Joe kissed his mother on the forehead. "Make me a pecan pie today, Mother."

"I have already planned to do that, son. You have a good day."

Ann kissed Mrs. Norton and said, "Just bake an old-fashioned chocolate cake for your baby daughter, please."

"Consider it done, dear. You be careful with Joe's car. And fix the church pretty."

"I will. Let's go, Joe."

"Dad, are you coming down to the store later this morning?" Joe questioned.

"Yes, about ten. It looks like rain, and I can't do anything here."

"Okay, good-bye to both of you." Joe and Ann drove swiftly toward town. Joe was anxious to see if Ben had prepared the store last night for the big day.

"I guess the rain won't hinder business too much today, because it's the last shopping day before Christmas," commented Joe.

"Yes. I still have some shopping to do," said Ann.

"Well, here we are. You be careful with this car, Ann, and don't work too hard."

She teased, "You must not think much of it, leaving it in my hands."

"Oh, I think a lot of it. The reason I'm letting you use it is because I think so much more of you than I do the car."

"I love you, too, handsome." She grinned and drove away.

When Joe stepped into the store, he could tell immediately that Ben had worked hard the night before. He was putting change in the cash register when Ben arrived.

"Five minutes late, as usual," he teased.

"Hey, fellow. Don't say anything to me. Louise and I worked until after eleven here last night," Ben retorted gaily.

"And you do have things looking swell, Ben. I thought I detected a woman's touch. How did you talk Louise into that?"

"Oh, she didn't want to stay home alone, and I was glad of her company. Did you have a good time last night?" asked Ben.

"I guess so. And I am grateful for what you've done. Sometimes I think I don't know how to adequately appreciate an employee like you," continued Joe.

"No, you really don't. If you did, you'd have fired me the day before I started working for you." Ben laughed heartily.

"This should be a profitable day, if the rain is not too heavy," Joe stated.

"Boy, you must have stayed up all night, from the looks of your eyes," observed Ben.

"Almost. When I got home, Ann was working on church decorations, so I helped her." He recalled again that eerie silence after Ann had teasingly said she'd be lucky to survive the holiday preparations.

"Ann's a hard worker," said Ben. "I know she'll have the church looking exquisite for tonight."

"I'm afraid she'll be so tired she cannot enjoy the program," mused Joe.

"Well, when Shep drives that new car out tomorrow morning, she'll forget all that. In fact, she'll probably faint," suggested Ben.

The first two hours of the day proved to Joe that this would be the best day of the year indeed. When Mr. Norton arrived at ten o'clock, Ben was at the computer and Joe was taking an order by phone.

"Hello, Mr. Norton," greeted Ben.

"Where's my Christmas gift, fellow?" asked Mr. Norton.

"My, I wish you hadn't asked that. All I have to offer is a few of these bolts around here, and they belong to your boy. And you know how he feels about them," Ben spoke in a mockingly serious tone.

"Yes, he wouldn't think of giving one to his poor old dad."

Joe had walked over. "Well, if he needed it, I'd give him one little bolt. But really, Dad, how're you feeling?"

"Fine. I'm looking for Santa Claus. And I think the rain is about to do me in. It's a slow drizzle, but it's pretty rough weather." He paused briefly. "I thought we would go over to Winston Motors, pay for the car, and sign the papers. I'll give you a signed check, and you complete it for whatever my half of the total is, son."

"Okay. Or I'll just pay for it and you can pay me back later."

Mr. Norton left and the boys went back to work. It seemed everyone in Winston came in to buy something, and Joe was glad to see each of them. By noon the rain had intensified and it was turning colder.

At three o'clock, Shep came in. "You fellows certainly look busy."

"It's getting colder out there, isn't it?" asked Joe.

"Yes, sir. It's freezing right now," Shep advised.

"You don't mean it!" exclaimed Ben.

"Yes, sir. That rain is freezing just about as soon as it falls. A lot of cars are stalling, too." He went on, "Joe, your dad came in and we completed the paperwork on Ann's car. It's in the back now."

"Have you serviced it?" asked Joe.

"No, I'll do that tonight after the Christmas program. It will take only a couple of hours," advised Shep.

"Why don't you get Joe to help you?" quizzed Ben.

"Good idea," laughed Shep.

Joe grinned as he sat down at the desk. "When Joe leaves this place tonight, he's going to concentrate on one thing only for a day or so."

"Reckon he's trying to get married, Ben?" asked Shep.

"He'd better hurry. In a few years, he'll be so old he'll have to take someone that nobody else would have," added Ben.

"Ben, how much did you tell him the license will cost him?" questioned Shep.

"Four dollars down and all he makes for the rest of his life," replied Ben.

After another round of guffaws, Shep said, "I'll get back across the street and see what the guys are doing. Joe, where's the radio you wanted me to put in Ann's car?"

"On that shelf next to you -- the M-328. Get it and save me the walk around there," said Joe.

Shep pulled down a box. "Is this a new model?"

"Yes. It's just like the one in my car. We have sold so many of them."

"Well, I'll see you boys tonight," called Shep, as he headed toward the door.

"Be careful on that ice," warned Ben.

As Joe became busy again, his thoughts of making his sister happy on Christmas Day were lost in the business rush. At five-thirty, Ben answered the phone and said, "It's for you, Joe."

When Joe finished helping a customer, he answered, "Hello."

"Joe, is that you?" He recognized the sweet voice of a special nurse at the hospital. However, he sensed tenseness in Sue's voice.

"Yes, madam, this is Joe. Don't tell me you have to work tonight and will miss the program."

"It's more serious than that, Joe. Can you come to the hospital right away?"

Joe frowned as he realized something truly was wrong. "What is it, Sue?"

"Don't get alarmed, Joe. Ann has been in an accident. The ambulance brought her in, and she's in serious condition. She will be out of the operating room soon, and I wanted you to be here."

Joe's heart pounded wildly. His voice croaked hoarsely, "What happened?"

"They said the car slipped on the ice and went over a steep embankment. I don't know the details, Joe. But I feel strongly that you should come be with Ann just as soon as you can."

Joe realized that Ann's condition was probably more critical than Sue had related. He replied, "I'll be there in a couple of minutes."

He replaced the receiver and turned a pale face to Ben and several customers who stood at the counter.

"What's wrong, Joe?" asked Ben quickly.

"Ann had an accident and is at the hospital in serious condition." His voice trembled and tears welled up in his eyes. "I've got to go there now, Ben. Can you take care of the store?"

"Of course, I can. Here are the keys to my car, but you take it easy on those icy streets. After I close, I'll come by the hospital. You stay with Ann. Now get gone," said Ben firmly.

Joe pulled on his coat as he went out the back door and was on his way. In five minutes, he was at the hospital. He spoke to the people in the first waiting room, then walked to the main hall. He saw Sue coming out of surgery. He wanted to go meet her, but his legs would not respond. She walked quickly to him, touched his arm, and said, "Joe, I'm glad you have come."

"How is Ann?" he asked.

"They will bring her out in about ten minutes and put her in room 32. Would you like to wait there?"

"Sue, you have never kept a secret from me, and you must not do so now."

Joe's voice was so pitiful that it broke Sue's heart. "Joe, they don't have any hope for Ann. But you must remember, God is our refuge and a present help in time of trouble. Come, I'll take you to room 32."

As Joe followed her mechanically, he could think of nothing but losing his sister.

"I must go back and help with Ann. We'll bring her here in just a bit. When I get off duty in about twenty minutes, I will come stay with her," promised Sue.

"Thanks, Sue." Joe slipped into a chair, bowed his head, and began to weep. Sue put a hand on his shoulder.

"Joe, don't do that. Ann needs you to be strong now." She spoke softly.

"Yes, I guess you're right," replied Joe, wiping the tears from his face.

Sue kissed his forehead tenderly. "Remember, dear. As long as there is life, there is hope -- especially when our trust is in God."

After she left, many thoughts raced through Joe's mind as he waited. He remembered the camaraderie he and Ann had shared the night before as they worked on her decorations. He recalled her comment about being lucky if she lived through all the festive preparations. And then he wondered if the heavy silence they had both felt had been an omen of things to come. Oh, surely Ann would be all right! She must! She was only sixteen -- she had so much living to do!

Soon the door opened and Sue entered, followed by an orderly who pushed Ann upon a gurney. They laid her on the bed, and Sue made her as comfortable as possible. Joe took one look at his sister and turned away. Ann's head was almost completely covered with bandages. Her face was so bruised, it was difficult to recognize her.

Dr. Blair came in and checked her pulse. He gave Sue several orders, then turned to Joe. "Hello, son." He placed a hand on Joe's shoulder.

"How is she, Doctor?"

"I wish I could tell you that Ann will be fine, Joe, but I cannot. Her body has been virtually crushed from her waist down, with extensive damage to her lower internal organs. Several ribs are broken and one lung is punctured. In addition, her spinal cord has been severed, and her brain is swelling rapidly." He paused, then added gently, "Joe, if Ann comes through this, it will be because of a Higher Power than we have here. However, I must be honest and tell you that, given the severity of her injuries, the kindest option might be to wish her Godspeed on her journey to her heavenly home. Unless God intervenes, I am afraid she would suffer almost unbearable pain if she survives. But she is about as close to me as she is to you, and I will be doing all that I possibly can for her."

"Thank you, Dr. Blair. I appreciate your honesty and your efforts."

"Since Miss Martin is a personal family friend and one of our best nurses, I'm leaving her in charge of this room. I will be in frequently to check Ann. We have called your parents, Joe, and they will be here soon."

After Dr. Blair left, Sue was busy with the patient, who was connected to several machines.

"Is she unconscious?" asked Joe cautiously.

"Yes, Joe. And I must give her another shot," advised Sue softly.

In about fifteen minutes, Mr. and Mrs. Norton arrived. Mrs. Norton had been crying. Mr. Norton's face was drawn into a tight frown. Sorrow had gripped their hearts, and they could only pray as they waited for the outcome. Mrs. Norton kissed the swollen lips of her daughter, then took Joe's hand. He led her to a chair where she collapsed wearily.

"What will we do, son?" she asked Joe tearfully.

"There is still hope, Mother," replied Joe bravely. He had regained his composure and knew he must be strong for his parents.

Mr. Norton stood motionless by the bed, looking at his only daughter. Tears slipped silently down his weather-beaten face. Joe had never seen his father weep, and that sight doubled the pain in his own heart.

Sue had slipped out unnoticed and now returned. "Here is something to make you feel better," she said to Mrs. Norton.

"Thank you, dear," responded Mrs. Norton, as she drank the contents of the glass Sue handed her.

Sue brought in more chairs and tried to make the family comfortable. However, Joe stood at the foot of the bed, seldom taking his eyes off Ann.

In about an hour, Ann stirred and opened her eyes. She looked around the room and called in a whisper, "Mother."

Those in the room could not believe she had spoken, considering the seriousness of her injuries. Joe thought surely God had granted them a miracle.

Mrs. Norton leaned over the bed, "I'm right here, dear, and here I'll stay."

"Where's Dad?" asked Ann.

Mr. Norton was on the other side of the bed. "Here I am, little girl."

"We've had a lot of good times, haven't we, Dad?"

"Yes, and we'll have some more soon," responded her father.

"Dad, I'm afraid not. I'm ready to go live with the Lord now." Ann's voice faded, and she lapsed into unconsciousness again.

Sue was surprised. She had certainly not expected Ann ever to speak again, and she knew Dr. Blair had not believed she would come out of the coma.

At seven-thirty, a different nurse came to the door and advised, "Mr. Shank wants to see you, Joe."

"Thanks, Mrs. Lane." Joe glanced down the hall and saw Ben. As they met, Ben asked, "How is Ann?"

"Not good, Ben. She has suffered such massive internal injuries that Dr. Blair does not offer us any hope." Joe's eyes were on the floor.

"As long as there's life, there is hope, Joe. You must remember that Ann loves and serves a God who is able to do all things."

"Yes, I know, Ben. And I have to believe He will do what is best. He always has," acknowledged Joe.

"They are postponing the Christmas program, and we are going to have an hour of prayer for Ann," Ben advised.

"You mean they know about the accident already?" questioned Joe, in surprise.

"Everyone in Winston knows, and the whole town is in sorrow. We all love Ann."

Joe thought aloud. "Perhaps they should go on and have the program. Some people may be disappointed."

"We couldn't possibly have the play without Ann," stated Ben.

Joe knew that no one could fill Ann's place with him. The two men stood in silence for a time, with Ben quietly offering his strength to his friend and employer, and Joe gratefully accepting it.

"I brought the money over here. Business was wonderful. We took in about fifteen thousand dollars today," advised Ben.

"That's good, but you take care of the money, Ben. I don't need to keep it here."

"I'll make a night deposit, if you wish, Joe."

"Fine, Ben. Before you deposit it, take your regular salary out, then take a thousand dollars as a Christmas present to you and Louise from Ann and me." His voice broke as he thought about how much he cared for Ben and Louise. He knew Ann felt the same way about this dear couple.

"That's too much, Joe. I appreciate all you do for me, but that's more than I'm worth," argued Ben.

"To me, Ben, you are worth more than the business itself. So do as I ask, and then make the deposit," Joe spoke firmly.

"Thank you, Joe. And you must know that I'll stand by you as a friend. After the service tonight, I will come back to the hospital. And we'll all be praying for Ann and the family."

"Thanks, Ben. I appreciate your stopping by."

Joe turned again toward room 32. Ordinarily, he would have been ecstatic to receive fifteen thousand dollars in one day. But tonight his heart was gripped by the iron hand of grief, and the money meant nothing.

When he entered the room, Sue was giving Ann another shot, and he noticed how tired she looked.

"Why don't you go somewhere and rest a little, Sue?" he asked.

"I can't, Joe. I will be here until something develops. Maybe she will revive again in a little while. I was hoping she would recognize you."

Joe was glad Ann had spoken to his parents earlier, but it troubled him that she had not recognized him. He tried to make himself believe that she did not see him. He told himself that she would be well soon, and then they could talk for a long time.

Dr. Blair came in at fifteen-minute intervals and checked Ann. His face wore a mask of sadness that he could not hide.

At eight-thirty, Pastor Jenkins arrived. He spoke comforting words to the family, nodded to Sue, then prayed for Ann. His prayer touched Joe's heart, and he felt a genuine respect for the devoted preacher. Before he left, the pastor assured the family he would be in a nearby waiting room.

Sue removed one of the needles from Ann's arm and pushed the glucose stand to the corner. She checked Ann's pulse and looked at Joe. He could detect that Ann might be making a change for the worse. He longed for help and comfort, but could find none.

At nine-thirty, Ann whispered Joe's name. He bent over her. "Here I am, little sister."

"Joe, I'm sorry I ruined your car," she whispered hoarsely.

"Don't worry about that, Ann. I'll get another car. You just hurry and get well."

Mr. and Mrs. Norton had joined Joe at her bedside. Ann swallowed painfully and looked into Joe's eyes. "I won't ever be well in this world, Joe. It is time to go to my eternal home."

"Don't say that, Ann. God knows how badly we need you," said Joe tearfully.

"God knows best, Joe. But I want you to promise me that you'll go to church and become a Christian, so we can all be together in Heaven. You must promise me, Joe."

Tears flooded Joe's face. "But, Ann, I need you to help me. I promise I will go to church. Ann, don't leave us. I promise I will go to church."

"I can go in peace now." Ann smiled at them, then turned her face to the wall. She saw Sue and whispered, "Be as good to Joe as I have wanted to be." Sue touched her face gently with one hand and pushed the call button with the other.

Mrs. Norton sensed the truth from the expression on Sue's face and began to pray aloud, "Oh, God. Please don't take my only daughter. It is more than I can bear."

In seconds, Dr. Blair appeared and hastily examined Ann. Pastor Jenkins also came in and tried to comfort Mr. and Mrs. Norton. Joe stood at the foot of the bed like a statue, hardly daring to breathe, staring into space.

But all efforts were in vain. Dr. Blair pulled the sheet gently over Ann's face, which now displayed perfect peace. He turned to Joe with tears in his eyes. "Joe, I did all that was in my power. But God knows best." Then the doctor turned to Joe's parents.

Grief raked through Joe like hot iron claws. He gazed unbelievingly at the still form under the sheet. He felt so alone. Then nausea overpowered him, and he staggered to a chair. When he came to, Sue was wiping his face with a damp cloth. She put a glass to his lips, and said, "Drink this, Joe. It will help."

He did, and soon felt he could stand. Shep Owen entered and took Joe by the arm. Joe looked again at the lifeless body on the bed. He knew that Ann had been swept into the presence of God, but giving her up was so difficult.

Sue touched his arm, "Joe, I'll be with you as soon as I can." Shep led him away.

"Son, be strong in this hour, for the sake of your mom and dad," advised Shep. They reached the waiting room where Pastor Jenkins and Dr. Blair tried to console his parents. Ben and Louise were also there.

"Joe, I have given your mother and dad a sedative, and you should get them home and to bed. And remember, they are depending on your strength, son," said Dr. Blair.

"I'll do my best, Doctor. Thank you for all you have done," replied Joe.

Dr. Blair turned to Shep, "Are you going to the farm with them, Shep?"

"Yes, I'll be there the rest of the night," responded Shep.

"Good. I'll be home if I am needed," advised the doctor.

Joe spoke to his parents. "Let's go home now and try to rest."

"Oh, how can we leave her, son? Things will be so different," sobbed Mrs. Norton.

"Yes, I know, Mother. But Ann is in a much better place now. And she would want us to find comfort in that." He spoke softly.

She clung to Joe's arm as he turned to his father. "Shall we go, Dad?"

In a dazed manner, Mr. Norton replied, "I hate to leave my only daughter, son. But I know there's nothing more we can do."

"Ben, you and Louise come by for a while," requested Joe.

"Yes, we're planning to do just that," said Ben, opening the door for them.

The rain had ceased just before dark, and the clouds were now flying toward the south. The moon peeped through quite often to illuminate the town of Winston. Sadness gripped the heart of the entire city, for there was no one more popular than Ann Norton.

The night air was cold, and the streets were still icy and dangerous. Joe drove straight home with his parents in the Shanks' car. Ben and Louise followed closely behind them in a taxi. Shep carried Mrs. Owen home, then came to the Norton farm. Pastor Jenkins and his wife came over, and several other friends stopped by. Joe put his parents to bed, and they were soon fast asleep under the influence of the sedative. Dr. Blair later called to see how they were and to advise he would stop by the next morning. Joe returned to the room where Ben, Louise, and Shep were talking quietly.

"Ben, when you and Louise get tired, the guest room is empty," he stated.

"Oh, we'll be all right, Joe," assured Louise. "Is there anything we can do for you?"

"No. I want to be alone for a while, if you don't mind. Shep, you may lie down in my room, if you like, and I'll be there after a bit."

"Sure, Joe. I'll turn in when I get sleepy. But you try to get some rest, too, son."

Joe walked out the back door and into the yard. He stopped near the fence under the apple tree. The leaves were gone and the moonlight revealed a brokenhearted young man. Joe gazed into the heavens, watching the dark clouds continue their eternal cycle. Tears streamed down his cheeks as he wept silently. He was unaware that the weather was extremely cold and his jacket very thin.

He felt Rags nudge his leg. "Rags, if you only knew about your master," whispered Joe. As though he sensed Joe's sorrow, the dog stood close to him, his tail tucked between his legs. His mournful eyes looked up at Joe, as if in understanding. Joe patted him lovingly for several minutes, then the big dog trotted off to the garage.

As Joe looked again toward the sky, he wished the dark cloud over his heart could pass as quickly as the storm clouds of the day. He became aware that someone was approaching, but he didn't turn to see who was joining him.

Sue had completed several reports and then driven directly to the Norton home. She had found Louise, Ben, and Shep, and they had told her Mr. and Mrs. Norton were asleep and Joe was outside.

She touched Joe's arm, and he turned. He had hoped it might be Sue. "Are you trying to catch pneumonia?" she asked.

"No. I'm not cold," he answered.

Sue wore a heavy navy coat over her uniform and a blue scarf around her head. Her face was tired and drawn, but she was anxious to comfort Joe. She pulled a small lace handkerchief from her pocket and wiped the tears from his eyes.

"I knew that I loved you, Sue, but I never realized how much until now," he confessed. He took her gloved hand in his own.

"I didn't know how much you meant to me until tonight, Joe."

"I can't understand why Ann had to go like she did. But if anyone in this world can fill the void in my heart, it is you, Sue."

"Ann believed that God had a purpose in it, Joe, and we must believe that, also. And I am sure there is no one who wants to try to fill the emptiness in your heart any more than I do."

Joe stretched out his arms and pulled Sue close to him. Her cheek pressed against his, and her body clung to him. This was the comfort Joe needed. He began to cry, and she didn't try to stop him. She knew it would do him good to get it all off his chest. She caressed his cheek and neck gently and whispered, "Joe, I love you so much. I know that God will work things out in our lives."

"Oh, He must!" sobbed Joe. "If I lose you, too, then just let me die!"

"Don't say that, Joe," Sue moved away from him, blushing as she realized what she had done. Though it was exactly as her heart had wanted, this was not a common occurrence in Sue's life.

"Let's go to the house, Joe, before you catch cold. You need some rest." She led him toward the back door. Joe felt much better, and he was grateful Sue had found him.

Ben and Louise had retired, and Shep had gone to Joe's room.

"I'll go home and get some rest, too," said Sue.

"Thank you for coming. It has meant so much to me, dearest."

"I'll be back in the morning. Promise me, Joe, that you will try to sleep."

As he held the door for her, he agreed, "I promise I'll try. I hope I dream of you tonight."

"Good night, Joe." She smiled tenderly at him.

Joe turned out the lights and went to his room, where he found Shep reading the Bible. "Shall I read a little Scripture, Joe, before we retire?"

"That would be fine, Shep."

Shep began to read from the twenty-third Psalm, "The Lord is my Shepherd, I shall not want . . . He maketh me to lie down in green pastures . . . ."

Never had this Psalm comforted Joe as much as it did now. The two men sat in silence afterwards until Joe spoke, "Shep, I want you to pray for me . . . ."

"I have been, and I will now, Joe."

The older man bowed his head and prayed aloud to God. Joe felt the earnestness and sincerity of his prayer. After praying for consolation for the Norton family, Shep prayed for Joe's salvation. But Joe hesitated about accepting Christ. He silently promised that he would try to be good and go to church. It seemed these two concessions were all he could make at this time. "Maybe some other time I will accept Christ," he said to himself.

After his prayer, Shep stretched out on the bed. Not another word was spoken between the two men, and eventually, they both slept.

Christmas Day was long and lonesome for Joe. Shep left about seven-thirty, and Ben and Louise soon followed. Some relatives had come to stay with Mr. and Mrs. Norton, and Dr. Blair also came to check on them.

Joe spent most of the morning walking through the pasture with Rags. Just about the time Joe would get lost in almost unbearable grief, the dog would bound away after a sparrow, barking with every breath. This would attract Joe's attention, and Rags would come to him for a friendly pat on the head. When they reached the winding stream, Joe threw sticks across it and watched Rags splash through the water to bring them back to him. When Rags would shake his body, the icy water would cause a chill to pass through Joe, but he didn't mind. He was thankful that Rags kept him occupied in something more pleasant that the present circumstances of his home.

He remembered that the family was to go to the funeral home at two o'clock. As he headed toward the house, he could not contain his tears. After everyone arrived at the funeral home, Joe looked at Ann only once. He realized that she was not inside that still form, but had gone to her reward. About seven o'clock, Sue came over for a short while.

The funeral was to be at three o'clock the next afternoon with Pastor Jenkins in charge. Joe was unable to sleep that night as he dreaded this final good-bye. By two-thirty, the church was packed and some folks had to stand. There were many, many arrangements of flowers. Pastor Jenkins began with the reading of Scripture. The church quartet sang, then the pastor prayed, and there was another beautiful song. Almost everyone shed tears, except Joe. His face was thin and pale. He breathed deeply, silently questioning, "How can this be, O God?!"

By five-thirty, the grave was finished and a lone figure stood among the flowers. Joe had asked Shep to leave him there for a while. With no one around to hear, he cried aloud, "Why, God? Why did You tear my little sister from us in such a cruel manner? You knew that we needed her, yet You took her, anyway. Why, God? I thought You were a just, loving God, but what is just -- what is loving -- about this? Where is the loving God that Mrs. Owen talks about? Where is the God of Sue Martin's faith? And, yes, where is the God of my parents?" Joe buckled to his knees among the flowers and angrily pounded the cold earth, as gigantic sobs ripped through his chest. He cried until he was too weary to cry any more, then rose and stood silently by Ann's grave.

He heard a twig snap and knew he was no longer alone. His heart beat faster as he listened to the light footsteps coming nearer. He knew it was Sue. When she reached him, she slipped her soft hand into his and squeezed it gently. Joe returned the affectionate greeting in the same manner.

"I had to come to you, Joe," whispered Sue.

"I thought you might, and I've been waiting," he replied.

"Joe, I've been doing a lot of thinking and praying. I have decided it is the Lord's will for me to say 'yes' to the question you asked me when we were at the lake."

His heart leaped within him, and he was speechless. He looked at Ann's grave, then at the western sky, then back to Sue's face. In the last moment of light, it seemed the most beautiful and loving face he had ever seen. Sue blushed beneath his gaze, then yielded to his eager arms as he pulled her body to his own.

"I'm so happy, Sue! But what about South America?"

"Some day it will be possible for both of us to go," she answered.

"That would be wonderful. I can go anywhere with you," stated Joe. Then tears of both sadness and joy began to flow down his cheeks. Sue held him gently, then dried his eyes again.

"I'm sorry Ann had to go, Joe. But I do believe that she would be as happy about this as we are."

"Yes, I know that's true, Sue. And I am so thankful for you." He looked into her eyes, then pulled her closer. As she tilted her face up to his, he covered her soft, sweet lips with his own.

Chapter III

Joe and Sue were married on Sunday afternoon, February fifteenth. The wedding was the social event of Winston. The church was beautifully decorated and filled to capacity. Joe had been a favorite among the people of Winston for many years, and Sue had gained numerous friends since her arrival. Joe was handsome in a white tuxedo, and Sue looked almost ethereal in the long, white gown which had been lovingly fashioned by her mother. Ben was Joe's best man, and Louise was matron of honor. Sharon served as bridesmaid. Don Drane's wedding music was his best performance ever. Pastor Jenkins performed the ceremony. As the bride and groom exchanged their vows, neither was ashamed of the tears of love and joy that slipped down their faces.

After the reception, the couple drove to Sue's home. As Joe's car had been declared a total loss by his insurance company, they drove the car that was to have been Ann's Christmas present. It was covered with signs of "Just Married" and "Long Live This Couple." A few cans and a cowbell were tied underneath the vehicle.

Sue hurriedly changed into traveling clothes while Joe put a couple of suitcases into the car for her. Soon they told the Martin family good-bye and drove toward the Norton farm.

Mr. and Mrs. Norton and Ben and Louise waited for them. As Joe and Sue stepped from the car, a tall Negro man stood near the dairy barn, dressed in a white shirt and striped overalls.

"Hey, Slim," Joe called and motioned for him to come closer.

Slim had worked for Mr. Norton for ten years and had grown very fond of the entire family. His heart had been broken when Ann had her fatal accident, but Slim loved Joe Norton more than any other white person on earth. Joe often teased him, but just as often, was doing some special favor for the elderly man.

"I know your religion won't permit you to do much more than milk cows on Sunday, Slim," said Joe teasingly. "But I do wish you would clean this stuff off the car before it dries."

"How do you do, Miss Sue," spoke Slim, as he bowed his head politely toward Sue.

"Hello, Slim," she replied softly.

"Yes, sir. I will fix this car up right for you two honeymooners," grinned Slim, showing sparkling white teeth with many gaps.

"Slim, you didn't think I'd ever get married, did you?" asked Joe.

"No, sir. But I'm glad you waited until now, 'cause I think you've got yourself a fine companion."

"Thank you, Slim," said Sue soberly.

"And, Miss Sue, you've got the best young man God ever made. He is the greatest friend old Slim has ever had," Slim went on solemnly.

Joe grinned, "Thanks, Slim. I'll pay you for that after you get the car cleaned."

They all laughed, and Slim took the car toward the dairy barn. In half an hour, Joe and Sue were ready to leave. Joe kissed his mother tenderly, "Make Dad behave himself while I'm gone."

"He will. I don't have too much trouble out of him. But do be careful, son. And you two have a wonderful honeymoon." Mrs. Norton hugged Joe affectionately.

"Don't work too hard, Dad," Joe cautioned Mr. Norton.

"Don't you worry about us, son. We'll be right here when you return. I am proud of you, and I believe you made the right decision today," advised Mr. Norton.

Ben had carried Joe's bags to the car, so Joe walked to where he and Louise waited.

Mrs. Norton held Sue's hand tightly as tears rolled down her cheeks. "My tears are for joy, Sue. Less than two months ago, God saw fit to take my only daughter. But today He has given me another, almost as sweet and lovely as the other. I want you to feel toward me the same as Ann always did, Sue."

"Thank you, Mother Norton. I can never fill Ann's place here, but I'll do my best to fit into the family. God bless you, and we'll see you soon."

Mr. Norton called after her, "Make that boy stop at all the gift shops and buy exactly what you want. This may be your only opportunity!"

"I'll take your advice, sir. And we'll send a postcard soon." She smiled at her father-in-law.

Sue was almost to the car when Ben wisecracked, "Joe, I hope you eat her up these next two weeks."

"Why?" asked Sue in amazement.

"Because in the months to come, he'll wish he had."

"Oh, you're a mean boy, Ben Shank." Though she was embarrassed, Sue joined in the laughter.

Joe commented, "Ben, I see you didn't eat Louise."

"No. And that's exactly why I'm giving you this warning," chuckled Ben.

"You'd better hush, Ben." Louise slapped his shoulder playfully.

"Let's go, Sue, before he gets unruly," suggested Joe.

They drove away as their friends waved and wished them well. When they returned two weeks later, they were even happier together.

For almost a year, Joe and Sue lived with Mr. and Mrs. Norton. Sue quit her job at the hospital, so she could do most of the work at home and let Mrs. Norton try to regain her health. Everyone got along well. Joe's business had escalated so that he considered hiring another man.

Joe had taken a very active part in church work, which Sue encouraged. He seldom missed a service, and he and Sue were Pastor Jenkins' standbys. Joe sang in the male quartet, he served as usher, and sometimes he led the prayer service on Wednesday night. The first six months that he and Sue were in charge of the missions program, the church paid twice as much money to missions than it ever had before. Sue and Joe talked often about going to South America.

On the first Monday of the following February, Shep Owen offered a suggestion to the church board. "Let's send Joe and Sue Norton to the mission field and let our church sponsor them."

Everyone agreed it was an excellent idea. They were well qualified, the church was able, and it was their duty to have a missionary on the field. It was decided that Pastor Jenkins would go to their home that night to tell them. If all the paperwork could be completed, they could sail the first of April.

When Pastor Jenkins arrived that evening, they were eating supper. Mr. and Mrs. Norton were visiting friends.

"Good evening, Joe and Sue," said Pastor Jenkins.

"Come in, sir," invited Joe, rising to greet the reverend.

"Have a bite to eat with us," offered Sue.

"No, thanks. I'll just sit here with you. I have already eaten."

"Well, how about some pie and a glass of cold milk?" enticed Sue.

He hesitated, then replied, "It's mighty hard to refuse that, when I know what a good pie you bake, Sue. But I'll wait until you two are ready for dessert."

As Joe and Sue continued eating, the three of them had a general discussion about church work. When the meal was finished, they all enjoyed dessert. Then Sue cleared the dishes and they retired to the living room.

"Let me state my business now," began Pastor Jenkins.

Joe and Sue looked at each other, but neither had time to speak before he continued. "We had a church board meeting today and decided we would do something for you two. Since you have started a definite program of missions in our church, financial support has increased tremendously. Therefore, we have decided to send you both to the mission field of your choice, and support you as long as you stay there."

"Oh, this is what we have hoped and prayed for so long, darling!" Sue exclaimed to Joe.

"Yes, I guess this is our chance," agreed Joe. "Tell us more about it, Pastor."

"Well, we know you both want to work as missionaries. We believe God is making it possible for you to fulfill His perfect will through our church. Your fare and your salary are in our treasury now. If you can get things ready, I will get your papers processed, and you can sail by April first."

"Oh, this is the best thing I have ever heard! I have wanted to complete my mission for God so long, and now the opportunity has come. Thank God for such a group of people!" Tears of gladness streamed down Sue's face. She touched Joe's arm, and continued, "Honey, this is the happiest moment of my life."

"Yes, dear, and I'm thrilled, too."

Pastor Jenkins sat watching the young couple. Sue was carried away with joy in her heart. She forgot everything else, and was laughing and crying at the same time. He noticed that Joe seemed a bit disturbed in his mind at this sudden turn of events. Of course, this was logical. A businessman couldn't leave town overnight. And Joe had to consider his parents, too.

Pastor Jenkins rose and said, "Well, I've told you the news. Think it over and let me know by Friday night when you want to go. But remember, Jesus is coming soon, and what we do for Him, we must do quickly." He left without another word.

"Joe, darling, I am so happy! This is what we have waited for almost thirteen months."

"Yes, dear. But I don't know if we can be ready by the first of April. I have so much to take care of before we can go," said Joe.

"I know, dear. But God will work it all out. In His providence He has made provision for us. I feel that we must go, even if we have to leave some things here undone," stated Sue.

"I guess you're right, but I must think it over. Now I have to go feed Dad's pigs before he gets back." Joe looked at his beautiful young wife, who stood close to him with her hands on his arms. "You are a pretty thing, little girl," whispered Joe.

"Tell me, Joe, that you will go to the mission field with me. I have waited for this, and I know it's God will for us. I'd rather die than not go," she spoke earnestly.

"I love you, Sue. And my greatest desire is to see you happy." Joe bent and kissed the warm lips of his bride, then turned and walked out.

Sue watched him go, then began to wash the supper dishes. She wondered if Joe really would get things ready to leave by April first. She felt as though she must go then or never.

Night had already settled when Joe went outside, but the darkness had been driven back by the silvery rays of the moon. It was chilly, but he hardly noticed. The crickets and katydids had started their gleeful chatter near the brook that flowed behind the house. The cows in the pasture had already retired for the night. The pigs squealed in the distance, because it was now an hour past their feeding time.

Joe threw some corn in the truck, then drove to the pig pen. As he threw the corn to the pigs, his mind was whirling. He knew Sue would not be happy here any more, yet it was hard to sell a business that he had dreamed of for many years. And he must consider his mother. Her health was bad, and about the time he got to South America, she might die. Then he could never forgive himself for leaving her. His dad also needed his help here at the farm.

Yet as Joe stood in the cool night air, he felt this might be the time for him to forsake business, father, and mother, and heed the calling of God. He gazed over the big pasture and said aloud, "I guess I'll have to get things lined up to leave as soon as possible."

When he returned to the house, he and Sue talked much about their plans. They did not tell Mr. and Mrs. Norton the news, though.

Late Friday afternoon, Sue was preparing the evening meal. Mrs. Norton had been out with her husband most of the day, and Sue had spent much time in prayer. Now she waited patiently for Joe, because her husband's decision was the important thing now. Sue was still happy over the plans, but somehow, she felt a sadness. If only she could look into the future for a moment. She realized the mission field was the only place she and Joe could be completely satisfied, because it was God's perfect will for their lives.

"We must go, and we must go soon," she muttered.

A car turned into the driveway and Sue glanced out the window. It was Joe. She placed a bowl of potatoes on the table, then turned to greet him.

After their usual embrace, she asked, "Have you decided what we are going to tell Pastor Jenkins?"

"Yes, dear. We are going."

"Oh, thank God! I know we will be happy the rest of our days." She kissed Joe affectionately on the cheek.

"But we may not be ready by the first of April. I've done some scouting today, and we probably cannot leave here until the first of May," said Joe, as he held Sue close to him.

"Well, any time, darling. Just so we are going soon. But do you reckon that will be too late?"

Joe replied firmly, "Don't say those words, honey. Every time I hear them, I shudder. I think they are the most horrible words ever spoken."

"They are sad words, Joe, and I hope we are never too late for anything in the work of God," responded Sue.

"Is supper ready?" Joe asked hungrily.

"Yes, sir. I've got my hubby's favorite dish, too."

"Every dish that your hands prepare is my favorite," he teased. "Where are Mother and Dad?"

"They left for town about three o'clock and said we shouldn't wait up for them."

"My, my. They really run around a lot these days," commented Joe.

About six o'clock, Pastor Jenkins came by on his way to a ministers' meeting. "Well, have you two decided to go?"

"Yes, I think we are, sir. But we cannot sail until May first," answered Joe.

The pastor stroked his chin and stared into space, his brow wrinkled. "Joe, is there any chance of sailing April first?"

"I'm afraid not, sir. We want to go, and we will go. But there are many things that I must attend to before we can sail. You see, besides Norton's Motor Parts, all this out here has been put into my hands."

"Yes, I know. But maybe some of us could take care of the work here after April first," suggested Pastor Jenkins. "What do you think, Sue?"

"Oh, I'd be ready tomorrow. The sooner the better for me. But I know Joe has to handle many details."

"Well, I'll get the papers for May first, but I surely wish you were going one month sooner. I believe we are living in the last days. What we do, we must do quickly. If not, I'm afraid we are going to be too late." The pastor spoke sorrowfully.

He didn't see the shadow that passed over Joe's face. Those words had been voiced again, and they were bitter to his soul.

After Pastor Jenkins left, Sue asked, "Do you suppose Pastor Jenkins is right?"

"I hope this is one time that he is wrong. But I'll try to rush the arrangements, and possibly we can leave by the middle of April," promised Joe.

"I hope so. But somehow, I just feel we should go the first of April," murmured Sue.

"We'll do our best, and I'm sure God will understand."

"Joe, let's call Pastor Jenkins and tell him to get the papers ready for April first," Sue spoke eagerly.

Joe sat in silence for a moment. "Honey, I would really like to do that, but I'm afraid we can't."

"Darling, if you feel we should, then let's do it. God will make the way," insisted the young woman.

"Dear, ten or fifteen days shouldn't make any difference," argued Joe.

Sue could tell that Joe was tired and worried. And maybe her feeling was just anxiety, and the joy of getting to fulfill the great desire of her soul. Yet she felt God was calling them to go at this particular time.

She rose, placed a hand on Joe's shoulder, and whispered, "I'm sorry if I was too persistent, darling. Why don't you stretch out on the couch for a while? You look bushed."

"I believe I will, sweet. Don't you worry. I'll get things arranged as soon as possible, and we'll go to South America for the rest of our lives and work for God."

"All right, dear." She kissed his brow. When she returned at eight-thirty, Joe was fast asleep. It had been an exhausting day for him physically and mentally, and he had finally relaxed from it all.

Sue knelt beside him and prayed for a long time. She then stood, smiled faintly at the sleeping form of the man she loved, and didn't awaken him until the next morning.

On April first, Sue was up early, as usual. When Joe came into the kitchen, he kissed her neck and said, "Well, this is the day we were supposed to sail."

"Yes, and I would feel much better if we were boarding the ship," replied Sue. Each day her anxiousness to depart for South America grew.

"I think I would, too," agreed Joe, "but I talked to Pastor Jenkins yesterday. He will have everything ready by the fifteenth. He is getting the paperwork changed from May first to the fifteenth of April. He was rather glad when I told him we would go earlier."

"I'm happy we're going, Joe. It's the best thing for both of us. And although they will miss us, our families are pleased, too."

"Yes, they are. I am truly thankful Mother is taking it the way she is," commented Joe.

He looked out the window into the cloudy sky. The clouds hung low, as if ready to pour out their contents upon instructions from their Maker. "My, this looks like a rough day."

"Oh, I know. This is the kind of day I would rather sleep through, but the Lord knows best," Sue spoke cheerfully.

Joe spent most of the morning in the office with Shep while Ben took care of the store. Joe had some ideas that might help to support them while on the mission field.

At eleven o'clock, he told Ben, "I need to run over to Pastor Jenkins' place for a minute. I'll be back very soon, and then you can go to lunch."

"Oh, I can't stop for lunch today. But I will appreciate it if you'll drop by the house and tell Louise to bring me a bite to eat. Our telephone is still out of order," advised Ben.

"Okay, but I'll be back as soon as possible." Joe went on his way.

Louise was very busy around the house. She had cleaned the carpets and waxed the floors and finished her lunch. She decided to take a bath before Ben came, so she could ride to town with him and do her shopping.

She undressed in the bedroom and pulled on a lightweight, rose-colored bathrobe. She stopped in front of the mirror. There was no denying that Louise Shank was a stunning woman. Her dark hair fell loosely around her shoulders and lay softly on the robe. She picked up a ribbon, pushed back her black hair to the crown of her head, and tied it there. This exposed the perfect profile of her slender neck and her tiny ears. If she were to enter another beauty contest, she would probably win.

Just as she started toward the bathroom, the doorbell rang. Who could it be? She hesitated, trying to decide whether to answer the door in her robe or quickly change clothes. The bell sounded again, so she decided to go as she was.

When Louise opened the door, her eyes glazed. Her heart began to pound hard within her breast, and her knees became weak. She was utterly speechless, for standing there with the screen door open and already coming in were the beady eyes, the hooked nose, and the fiendish grin of Jack Drowd.

He stepped inside, and laughed. "I've been watching you, bathing beauty. And I've come to pay you a visit."

Louise backed into the hall. Drowd followed her. She touched the telephone, but remembered it was out of order. Oh, why, why had the telephone company not repaired it?!

"Get out, Jack Drowd! Get out of my house, or I will kill you!" screamed Louise.

He laughed bitterly. "You almost killed me when you broke my heart by marrying that weakling you call your husband."

"I hate you, Jack, and God is my witness!"

"You are a beautiful thing when you are angry, Louise. I have always known that," purred Jack, as he feasted his lustful eyes upon the embarrassed form of the lovely girl who stood trembling before him.

Louise realized she had backed into a corner of the hallway and was trapped. There were no neighbors at home today, and Ben wasn't due for another hour. Then she had an idea.

"Listen, Jack Drowd. I want to tell you something. Since I went with you, I have made things right with God. I'm living for Him these days, and . . ."

"Shut up!" snarled Drowd. "You may have made things right with your God, but you never made them right with me! Ever since that night we spent in the little cabin, I've sworn to be with you again. So here I am, darling. And you surely look like you were waiting for me."

The memories of that night flooded Louise's mind. Oh, the pain, sorrow, and grief that night had caused her. Even now, it sickened her. Darkness threatened to envelop her, but she fought it, praying silently to God for help.

Drowd came closer and stretched out an arm for her. She drew back, but the wall refused to allow her out of his reach. He caught her by her left arm. She tried to scream, but no sound came from her mouth. Her eyes caught a glimpse of his passion-riddled face. His thin lips were parted slightly, revealing his yellow teeth, and his eyes were like balls of fire. His jaw was set, and

Louise knew there was no good intention in this wicked man's mind.

Jack Drowd's right hand reached up, caught the collar of the bathrobe, and stripped it from her shoulder, exposing her breast. Drowd laughed hoarsely, then snatched the robe from her right shoulder. Louise stood cowering in fear before this fiendish devil, bare to her waist. She realized that darkness was descending upon her. She felt him pull her body close to his and felt his hot breath upon her neck. Mercifully, the blackness overcame her, and she was conscious no more.

Just as consciousness was ebbing out of Louise, Joe Norton parked his Oldsmobile behind Jack Drowd's car in front of Ben's home. He stepped out of his car hurriedly, concerned that Drowd's vehicle was there. Many things flashed through Joe's mind as he rushed to the large picture window. In the doorway that led from the living room to the hall, Joe saw Drowd pulling Louise's half-clothed, struggling body to his own. Joe analyzed the situation in a split second and knew that Drowd was up to no good with an innocent woman. In another split second, he raced across the porch, kicked the front door open, and rushed inside. As he ran across the living room, he cried, "Drowd, let go of that girl!"

Drowd was startled by the invasion. As Joe cried out, he dropped the now-limp form of Louise, and she sagged to the floor.

As Drowd turned to meet the onrush of his visitor, Joe's left hand caught him by the collar. A hard fist smashed into Drowd's face, knocking him to the floor. He leaped up, but Joe caught him again, and dragged him into the living room. He realized the hall was too small to fight in, and he was worried they might hurt Louise.

Both men struggled for victory. One fought because he had been caught in a dirty deed and was trying to save his skin. The other fought to appease the hot anger that an old grudge produced and to avenge what Drowd had done to one of his closest friends. In Joe's mind, he could avenge some of the hurt that Ben and Louise had suffered.

Drowd snarled and hissed like a wild beast, as he lashed out with both fists. Joe fought with the stealth of death itself. His eyes were glued to the livid face before him. Every muscle in his body was tense. He was calling on all his strength, for he knew Drowd would kill him, if he could.

Joe was in much better physical condition than Drowd, but Drowd was as quick as an oiled cat and as slippery as an eel. Joe finally cornered him and hurled a hard fist into his mouth. As Drowd began to fall, his hand touched a table lamp that had a heavy metal base. Joe rushed to finish him off, but Drowd leaped up and smashed the lamp across Joe's head. Although Joe saw the blow coming, he was off balance and could not dodge it. Upon impact, he felt a sick, nauseating feeling in the pit of his stomach. His eyes blurred and his knees became weak. Drowd screamed with triumph and rushed toward the staggering Joe with the lamp upraised to strike again. One more blow would finish Joe Norton.

In the split second that it took Drowd to make the two steps to where he was reeling, Joe relived the past few minutes. He saw the lovely form of an innocent girl in the grasp of a brute, then he saw her slip to the floor. Joe's love for Ben and his wife cleared his vision in a twinkling of an eye and pumped a new flow of blood through his veins. He felt fresh strength in his muscles, and when Drowd started the downward stroke, Joe was ready for him.

He stepped quickly aside, and as Drowd's arm grazed his shoulder, he seized it with both hands. He twisted with all his might. Drowd let out a cry of surprise and pain, as his arm was ripped out of its socket at his shoulder. He had not expected Joe to recover so soon. His face was grimaced in horror, but he could not surrender to this young man whom he hated so much and had been so close to defeating. He grabbed a knife from his pocket, opening it as he pulled it out. Everyone was afraid of Drowd with a knife. He ran toward Joe, his eyes set in a steely stare, with the knife extended.

Joe now seized the lamp that Drowd had wielded a moment before, but he was too late for the desperate Drowd. Drowd sank the blade deep into the upper part of Joe's left shoulder. Joe wrenched away from the knife and it tore out of his flesh. Blood began to pour down his side, and he knew he must end the fight soon. He grabbed Drowd's wrist and twisted with every ounce of strength remaining in his left hand. Then he crashed the lamp base across the bony skull of Drowd. Drowd screamed in pain and tried to tear away from Joe. But Joe was half blind with fury now and weak from the loss of blood. He raised the lamp again and struck the forehead of Drowd with all his might. Drowd's eyes colored, he sank to the floor, and a dark pool of blood began to ooze from his nose and mouth. Never again would Drowd torment an innocent woman.

A tired Joe Norton turned to the form in the hallway. He threw the lamp on the floor, pulled a sheet from a bed, and covered Louise. Then he lifted her in his arms and placed her on the bed. He paused just long enough to see that she was breathing, then ran to call for help. As he went through the living room, he stopped a second and stared at the crumpled body of Drowd. Recalling that Ben's telephone was not working, he rushed toward his car and frantically dialed 911 on the cellular phone he had installed only last week. As he waited for an answer, he realized his life's blood was slipping away. When his call was answered, he could only choke out "301 Winchester." He then fell unconscious, half his body in his car, half on the ground. A pool of blood was beneath him.

In less than five minutes, an ambulance and a police car pulled alongside Joe's car. The blood had almost stopped flowing from Joe's wound, and the emergency medical technicians knew they must get him to the hospital quickly. As they loaded him into the ambulance, police officer Harry Stanton followed the trail of Joe's blood into the Shank house. He found the body of Jack Drowd in the disarray of the living room. He noted the blood on the floors and walls, then he stepped into the hall. From there, he saw Louise lying on the bed. He radioed back to the station to request the police chief to come, and also to call an ambulance for Louise and a hearse for Jack Drowd. As he waited for their arrival, he took pictures of the scene, never touching anything in the house.

When Chief Jim Peters arrived, he looked long and hard at the body of Drowd. The man had caused lots of trouble in Winston, but it was all over now. After both bodies were removed, one to the hospital and one to the morgue, Chief Peters left Harry Stanton to complete the investigation. He went to the store to tell Ben what he had found.

Ben went immediately to the hospital to be with Louise. He was confused, but he knew he must wait for some explanation from Louise or Joe.

Shep locked the store and went to the Norton home to tell Sue the news. She wept as she changed clothes. She was unable to control her tears as they drove to the hospital.

"Sue, I don't know what's happened. But whatever it is, you can be sure that Joe did the best thing he could. He needs you, so please calm yourself before we get to the hospital. You'll be the first person he asks for when he regains consciousness."

"I know, Shep. And I'll be okay. It's just such a shock."

Louise regained consciousness thirty minutes after Ben arrived at the hospital. When she realized where she was, she gripped Ben's hand and began to cry. The nurse saw her condition and gave her a sedative. Ben did not question her, and all she said to him was, "Thank God, I am safe with you, dear!" In a few minutes, she was asleep.

At three-thirty that afternoon, after receiving several pints of blood, Joe opened his eyes. He stared blankly at the ceiling. Sue and his parents were in the room, and Sue moved closer to his bed. She touched his fevered brow with her cool hand.

Joe turned toward her and smiled faintly. "I've been waiting to see you, honey. I was almost too late today." He spoke forlornly.

Sue kissed his bruised face. "Don't talk now, dearest. You can tell me all about it when you are stronger."

"You'll stay with me, won't you, Sue?" he asked.

She reassured him, "I wouldn't leave you for anything."

Joe realized he was very weak. He slept again, but Sue stayed by his bedside all night. The next morning he wanted to go home, but Dr. Blair thought differently.

The doctor released Louise into Ben's care. Unable to return to their own home, they were going to the Norton farm to rest for a few days. Ben stopped to see Joe briefly, but the doctor thought it best that Louise and Joe not see each other for another day.

At nine o'clock that morning, Chief Jim Peters, along with the city's detective, Ray Mace, came to see Joe.

"Hello, Joe," said Chief Peters.

"Hi, Jim," responded Joe.

"How are you feeling?" asked Ray Mace.

"I'm okay, Ray, as long as I can keep my girl close to me."

The men had already spoken to Sue. They had advised they wouldn't be long and she should keep her seat.

"Do you feel like telling us what happened yesterday, Joe?" asked the chief.

Sue listened as Joe told the story. Neither of them had mentioned the trouble before now, and she was anxious to know exactly what had happened.

Joe began his story at the store where Ben had asked him to take a message to Louise on his way to see Pastor Jenkins. He ended it with his call to 911.

"And the next thing I knew, here I was with a pretty woman holding my hand," concluded Joe.

Neither of the men asked Joe a single question. Ray had recorded Joe's statement, and as he finished, he turned to Jim Peters and said, "This matches the girl's story perfectly."

"I don't doubt Joe Norton's word. Drowd is just out of the way, and Joe saved a fine woman from shame and disgrace," replied Chief Peters coolly.

"What happened to Drowd?" asked Joe.

"He's dead," answered the chief.

Joe frowned deeply, and sorrow pervaded his countenance. He felt ill again. He lay in silence a long time. The two men left and yet Joe remained silent. While Sue was arranging flowers and trying to make him comfortable, his mind was in turmoil. It didn't make a man feel good to know he was a killer, even if the victim deserved to die.

Joe was released from the hospital the third day. There was a preliminary hearing of the case on the fourth day. Joe was dismissed a free man. Louise and Ben thanked him over and over for what he had done.

As he was not to work in the store for at least two weeks, Joe loitered around the farm. He carried his arm in a sling, so there would be no pressure on the wound until it healed.

But since he was hospitalized, Joe had become a different person. His behavior was now strange, distant, and reserved. No one could understand him, not even Sue. When she asked him about going to the mission field, he always gave her a sharp, harsh answer that sent her to her room weeping and praying for God's intervention. Joe didn't go to church at all. At first, Sue thought he was sick. Then she realized something worse had come over him.

On April 25th, Pastor Jenkins came to see Joe and Sue about going to the mission field. Joe told him that he was not sailing May first and didn't know if he would ever sail for a mission field. The pastor pleaded with Joe to change his mind, but he only shook his head. His mother's soft voice had no effect on his decision, nor did Sue's pleading alter his position.

"Joe, you had better change your mind, boy, because it is God's will for you and Sue. I don't believe it will be much longer before Christ returns. Then it will be too late to go," warned Pastor Jenkins.

Those words "too late" sank into Joe's brain. Before tonight, they had held a pathetic sadness, but now they infuriated him. He glared out the window, wishing he could just be alone.

"Sue may go, if she pleases, and I'll support her. But I am not going," he stated sharply.

"What is the matter with you, Joe?" asked Sue.

Joe stood and glared into the stricken face of his young wife. "Nothing, my dear. Nothing at all. But did you ever kill a man?"

His question cut the air like a steel whip. Everyone was silent, aghast. Sue then broke into tears and ran from the room. Pastor Jenkins could only clear his throat. Joe turned on his heel and walked out into the inky blackness of the night. For a solid month, loneliness was his constant companion.

On Sunday morning, the third of May, Sue sat at the side of the bed, holding Joe's hand. "Are you going to church with me, dear?"

"No, Sue. I think I'll just stay in bed. I feel tough and I didn't sleep too well last night."

Sue didn't insist. When she was ready to leave, she kissed Joe's mouth and said, "Be sweet, darling. I'll miss you on the pew beside me." Joe didn't answer, but her words sank like stones into his heart.

Pastor Jenkins preached on "God's Perfect Will." It was a stirring message, especially to Sue. After the service, she felt a strong urging to tell Pastor Jenkins that she would go to the mission field alone if it could be arranged. She started in his direction, then thought about Joe. If she left him, he might never get back to the church. As she stood trying to decide, Mr. and Mrs. Norton got ready to leave, so she walked out with them. She went on home to Joe, but she very much wanted to tell Pastor Jenkins that she would go alone to the place where she would be in God's perfect will.

When Sue reached the farm, Joe was sitting in a chair. He stood and pulled Sue close to him. "Honey, I've been a bad fellow this past month, I know. I haven't wanted to be, but something made me. Please forgive me for the way I have treated you."

Sue was surprised, but very pleased. "Darling, I couldn't hold anything against you." Joe covered her lips with his, and held her to him tightly. This was the first time in a month that he had spoken a kind word to her, and Sue cried tears of joy. The two were happy again, but they were still not in God's perfect will.

That afternoon while Mr. and Mrs. Norton rested, Joe and Sue walked hand in hand over the farm. They laughed and talked just as they had a few weeks ago. It seemed that Joe had pushed the tragedy of his fight with Drowd into the back of his mind and was now the same likable man he had always been.

When Sue prepared for church that night, Joe did also. Sue felt her prayers had been answered. When they arrived at church, many of Joe's old friends welcomed him back. In his heart, Joe was glad to be there. Sue sang in the choir, but he remained in the congregation. When the choir came down, Sue told Joe that she and Louise were scheduled to sing.

"I'm glad. That will help me a lot," whispered Joe. The girls sang "Redeemed" and their voices blended melodiously. Pastor Jenkins preached on "The Ever Imminent Coming of Jesus Christ." He preached as if

Christ would come that very night. The Spirit of God moved upon the entire congregation. Many things ran through Joe's mind, while Sue sat beside him, weeping. She had wanted to go to the mission field, but she figured there would be days ahead for that.

The four Nortons went home together. While they had refreshments, they discussed the service. "I surely want to be ready to go when Christ comes," said Mrs. Norton.

"If we are in His perfect will, like Pastor Jenkins preached this morning, it will be a wonderful time," said Mr. Norton.

"And what if a person isn't in God's perfect will?" asked Joe.

"Tribulation will be upon him, son. The most terrible days this world has ever known will come after God takes His church," replied his father.

"It certainly makes you search your life when you hear a message like that," commented Sue thoughtfully.

"Yes, it does," agreed Mr. Norton. "Well, let's have prayer and get to bed. I have to get up early tomorrow."

They all knelt around the table and Mr. Norton prayed a heartfelt prayer. Sue whispered her petition, and Joe was lost in thoughts of the second coming. He was afraid he was not in the perfect will of God. What if Christ should come this night? Then his father said "Amen" and his thoughts were turned in another direction.

Joe and Sue talked a long time after they retired to their room. Sue felt strange and lonely, and as though something was about to happen. "No, Joe is getting back on the right road now," she told herself. Yet she lay there long after Joe was snoring, wondering what was ahead of them. Pastor Jenkins' message stayed on her mind. She tried to pray but felt no spirit of prayer.

The burden grew so heavy upon her that she couldn't bear it. She broke into tears and sobbed softly on her pillow for several minutes. "I must go to South America and take Joe with me. If Jesus should come, He will look for us there. Oh, we must go! If we are left when Christ comes, how will we make it? Oh, God, spare us and help us to go."

Then the burden left Sue and the strangeness vanished. Her pillow wet with tears and her body damp with perspiration, she turned her face to the wall and slept.

At six-thirty the next morning, Sue dragged her weary body out of bed. It seemed she had slept only minutes. Fifteen minutes later, Joe followed her to the kitchen.

"I wonder why your parents are not up yet," observed Sue.

"I don't know. I'll see about them." Joe knocked on their bedroom door and called, but there was no answer. He repeated this action in vain. He turned the knob and thought his eyes must be playing tricks on him. The bed had been slept in, but no one was there. His father's clothes lay on a chest. A drawer in his mother's dresser was open, but Mr. and Mrs. Norton were gone.

"They aren't here, Sue. I guess they went for an early ride." He came back to the kitchen where Sue was preparing breakfast.

"Their car is here," said Sue, looking out the window.

Joe walked to the dairy barn, but he found Slim alone. "Have you seen Dad this morning, Slim?"

"No, sir. I was wondering if he overslept," replied Slim.

"No, I don't think so. Neither he nor Mother are in the house."

"Well, I don't know where they would have gone this time of morning," spoke Slim, his voice getting higher as his concern grew.

"Come here, Joe," cried Sue, as Joe came out of the barn. He could tell from her voice that she had discovered something. As he entered the house, he heard the radio.

"Listen, Joe, listen!" She began to cry as Joe embraced her.

"What's the matter, dear?" asked Joe tenderly.

"Listen to the radio, Joe. Listen to what they're saying."

> 'NEWS FLASH: Thousands of people mysteriously vanished off the face of the earth last night. We have been unable to determine what has happened. But whatever happened, we believe it took place around midnight. Hundreds of automobiles crashed into banks, trees, telephone poles, and buildings. All we know is that there are wrecked cars and no drivers. Thousands of bedrooms are vacant. Neighbors are searching for neighbors, friends for friends, relatives for relatives. But they are nowhere to be found. This whole earth is in an uproar. No business has opened in the nation today. One minister stood on the steps of our Capitol and cried to the thousands gathered there: "Christ has come and claimed His own. And because we had not accepted Him or were not in His perfect will, He has left us to go through the terrible days of tribulation. We are too late, too late to

receive the greatest blessing a human could ever enjoy." When this minister finished, churches began filling up with people who are seeking God. This is the latest report on this matter. We will bring you further developments as they occur.'

Joe and Sue stood as though paralyzed. "It happened, Joe. Jesus came last night and took your parents and all those who were ready. I am so thankful that Ben accepted Jesus two weeks ago. Oh, that I could die, instead of having to live now." Sue spoke with exceeding sorrow.

"But, darling, why did He not get you? You are the best person in the world," Joe spoke in disbelief.

Sue turned a tearstained face to her bewildered husband. "I believe Jesus looked for us in South America. We were not there, in His perfect will. He made the way for us to be there, but we wouldn't go. Now, it's too late. Too late to do anything about it."

Joe stared out the window. Those words "too late" beat upon his soul. He had been too late for many things in his life, but now he sorely wished he had not been too late in performing God's will. And it was bad enough that he should have missed the rapture himself, but he had caused Sue to miss it, also. He tried to comfort her. But she felt her heart could never be comforted until it rested in peace with God.

"Let's go to the church, dear," she whispered.

"Sue, I am so sorry I caused you to miss the rapture," sobbed Joe, with tears coursing down his face.

She looked at him sternly. "Joe Norton, don't you ever say that again. Yes, we missed it. And now we have to wait until God sees fit to take us another way. It may be a cruel way, but remember, Joe, anything will be worth enduring to see Jesus face to face."

Joe kissed her brow and thought, "What a wonderful, wonderful girl."

"Yes, let's do go to the church and pray," he suggested to Sue.

When they arrived, the church was filled with people, kneeling and calling upon God. Some of them Joe had never seen inside a church.

Sue went toward the ladies' prayer room. Her mind was so troubled that she knelt in silence for a long time. She felt she must identify why she was not taken in the rapture. She had been taught that every Christian on earth at the time of the rapture would be caught up to Jesus. She knew she was not in South America in God's will, but she also realized she would have been there if she could have persuaded Joe. So she did not truly feel this was why she had missed the rapture.

As she knelt, her mind wandered back over her entire life. She remembered many Sunday School lessons she had studied, many church-related activities she had participated in, many good deeds she had done, and an untold number of worship services she had attended. As her mind considered her past life, she realized now that there had been no deliberate, definite acceptance of Christ as her Lord and Savior. There was no time, no date, that she could point to and say with certainty that at that precise moment, she had been saved. She vaguely remembered shaking former Pastor Williams' hand and joining the church as a small child. At the time, she had thought that was salvation. She froze in shock as she understood that she had merely presumed salvation based on a genuine desire to do right. She had assumed a religious mindset, rather than experiencing a personal encounter with Jesus Christ.

Sue felt her body was literally paralyzed as she realized she had placed her trust in good works, and good works had not saved her.

Numbness permeated her entire being as she knelt in dazed silence. After several minutes, hot tears of disbelief and then regret gushed down her face, and bitter was the pain in her heart. If only she could call back the days. She would gladly have made public profession and acceptance of the King of Kings.

But, alas, she was realistic enough to know that she could only go forward from this point. And at that very moment, Sue Norton truly became a Christian. She prayed humbly for guidance and strength during the dark days that undeniably were ahead, and she pledged her allegiance to Jesus Christ. Although she knew the future would be difficult for those who accepted the Lord after the rapture, she felt a genuine peace in her soul.

Joe had stood in the rear of the church for a while. He had noticed that no one was at the store when they passed. He felt certain that Ben and Shep were both gone with the Lord. For Sue's sake, he hated himself for not going to the mission field when God had made the way. He felt tremendous guilt because he blamed himself for Sue's missing the rapture. He knelt beside a pew and began to cry and pray for her. He wished there could be a better way for her than to have to endure the tribulation ahead. But the more Joe prayed, the sicker he felt and the greater his fear of the future became.

He walked out to the sidewalk where many people were coming and going. He felt so ill he thought of going to the hospital, but remembered that someone had said it was packed to capacity with those who had suffered heart attacks or nervous breakdowns when they realized their loved ones were gone. Unaware of Sue's disarming discovery about the state of her soul, he wondered why she was staying in the ladies' prayer room so long.

When she joined Joe at last, she asked, "Are you ready to go home, dear?"

"If you are, honey," he replied, taking her arm and heading toward the car.

After they returned home, they talked of the future. Sue knew more about the Bible than did Joe. She spent much time explaining what was ahead of them and advising Joe what to do or not do.

"Whatever happens, Joe, don't lose contact with God. It will be terribly hard at times, but stay true. It is the only way of escape."

For a while, there seemed to be a great revival in Winston, but so many of the church people were gone. Pastor Jenkins no longer was there to preach a soul-stirring message from the Word of God.

For three to four months, people continued to flock to the church. There was a wonderful spirit of love in Winston. Jim Peters didn't make a single arrest, which proved there had been a change in the lives of the citizens. But by the fifth month, the crowds began to dwindle. It seemed people forgot the great event that had taken place. Only a few stayed in an attitude of worship daily.

Sue Norton refused to forget that she had missed the rapture. She would not allow her faith in God to waver, because she knew it was her only hope.

The first month after the rapture, Joe had sold Norton's Motor Parts to Winston Motors, the company where Shep had worked. He took a big loss, but money meant very little to him now. He felt he needed to be with Sue at the farm to offer protection and counsel. The second month, he and Sue had tried to book passage for South America. Though the burden of the work had left Sue, she still wanted to see if she could do something there for God. But again, they were too late. No Protestant missionary was allowed to leave the United States. So Joe and Sue decided to settle down at home and wait until God would deliver them from the treacherous days ahead.

By the seventh month, only a half dozen people met in the church. Sue and Joe were always there, though sometimes it seemed Joe went primarily to keep her company. A terrible spirit of hatred and jealousy settled over the country. Cities were burned, riots broke out, rivalries developed, former friends struggled to the death in the streets. No one dared to try to stop the trouble. Crops ruined in the fields for lack of rain and attention. By the ninth month, men were killing each other so fast they didn't take time to bury the dead. The streets of Winston were littered with corpses every hour of the day and night. No town was free from peril and danger. All men felt the evil grip of an unseen, terrible monster that incited them to kill.

Joe escaped all this trouble by staying home with Sue, except when they went to church. He carried a .38 revolver with him everywhere. He didn't want to use it, but he didn't want wicked men to molest or kill his wife.

Joe's faith was weaker than Sue's. He still wanted to depend upon himself to do things. He wanted to deliver Sue because of his great love and admiration for her. Sue prayed long and hard for their deliverance. Joe prayed for Sue, but his mind was so confused that he couldn't concentrate very long on God. Yet he felt he and Sue would need divine protection in the near future.

One dark night, Joe and Sue sat on the lawn discussing the terrible situation. A red glow appeared in the sky from the direction of downtown Winston. Joe leaped to his feet, exclaiming, "My, the whole town must be on fire!"

"Oh, no! But I'm afraid it is," agreed Sue.

"Let's go see about it," suggested Joe.

Sue hesitated, then said, "Let's not, dear. If the city is on fire, we can't stop it. Bad men have done it, and we might get into serious trouble. I feel that we should stay here."

"Okay, honey. You know best. But oh, I hate to see it burned."

The young couple stood in the silence of the night and watched the red glow. At times they saw flames leap above the treetops. Though the fire was a mile away, Joe and Sue perspired as if they were close to it. How it hurt to see their hometown destroyed. "Men have no respect for anything these days," growled Joe.

"That's true. The power of Satan has overcome these men, and he makes them do these awful deeds."

While they stood, a car turned into their driveway. Joe pushed Sue behind an evergreen bush, then stepped close to her. His right hand was upon his pistol.

"Joe." It was a familiar voice, but at that one word, Joe could not recognize it.

"Joe, are you there?" The occupant of the car sounded the horn.

"It's Jim Peters," whispered Joe to Sue.

"Yes, I'm here," Joe answered coldly.

"Well, come here, and let me talk to you a minute," called the chief.

"Get out of your car so I can see you, if you want to talk to me," Joe responded.

"Joe, don't tell me that you don't even trust me," said Chief Peters, as he opened his car door and stepped out.

"No one trusts anyone these days," reminded Joe. "Is anybody with you?"

"No, I'm alone, Joe," replied Jim.

"Okay, Jim, you may talk. But if you touch that gun of yours, I'll kill you in a heartbeat." Joe stepped from behind the bush.

"Joe, I haven't come to harm you. I am here to ask for your help."

Sue felt a cold sweat come over her. She had never heard Joe use that tone of voice. She had felt every muscle in his body tense, and she knew that Joe would have killed before being killed. And she didn't want that. Now this rough lawman was asking for Joe's help. What could this mean? Sue prayed silently as the police chief continued.

"Joe, the entire nation is fighting. War and bloodshed have come to our homes. Yonder burns the city that we both loved so much. As you know, a great number of our armed forces are in other lands combating terrorism, and we only are left to protect our country. I've been asked to get every man who is able to carry a gun to try to maintain law and order in this area. I want you to go with me."

"I can't do it. I must stay with my wife and protect her," Joe spoke curtly.

"Joe, unless we stop these men, they will overrun everything. They will kill you and molest Sue anyway. The place to stop them is out there, not here. And they are too many for you to fight alone," pleaded Jim.

Sue stepped from behind the bush and came to Joe's side. Jim Peters pulled off his cap and greeted her, "Good evening, Miss Sue."

"Hello, Jim. You've come to take Joe away from me, have you?"

"I wish I could say 'no,' Sue, but please don't think I'm cruel. I'm doing this for the good of us all. This world has gone mad and we must protect our women."

"When do you want me?" asked Joe, after several minutes of contemplation. He wanted to stay with Sue, but he knew he couldn't fight the mob alone. And he wouldn't mind dying, if he could know that Sue was safe.

"I'll wait fifteen minutes. You won't need to carry a thing with you. I'll give you supplies when we get to the warehouse. There will be about three hundred men waiting for us."

"I'll be ready," said Joe, as he turned away. He called Slim from his little cabin behind the dairy barn. While Slim was coming, he went inside the house and brought out several boxes of shells.

"Slim, I've got to leave for a while. I want you to guard Miss Sue with your life. If anything happens to her, I will hold you responsible." Slim knew Joe Norton was not teasing now.

"Mister Joe, if anything happens to Miss Sue, it will be after I have crossed over," he promised solemnly.

Slim was dismissed and Joe embraced Sue. They clung to each other tightly. "This is the saddest moment of my life, darling," whispered Joe.

"Mine, too, dearest, but God still lives and He will bring you back to me." Sue choked back tears as she spoke. "It's the best thing for both of us."

"Yes, but remember that if I never see you again, you are all there is or ever will be to me. I love you, darling, more than all this world. And I'm sorry for the heartaches I have caused you."

Sue didn't answer but lifted her face to his. A ray of moonlight crossed her face and held Joe spellbound at her beauty. Wet eyelashes, flashing eyes, tumbling blond hair, and soft lips. Joe kissed her long and hard, and embraced her as long as possible.

"Joe, I hate to rush you," said Jim Peters.

"I'm ready, Jim."

"We have to move from headquarters at midnight. You will be second in command, and we have lots to discuss."

Joe spoke, "Sue, go inside, lock the doors, and stay there. Don't open to anyone except Slim until I return. Good-bye, you wonderful girl." He squeezed her hand and turned to go.

"Bye, darling. I believe God will bring us together again."

Joe departed with Jim Peters. Sue saw him turn and look back only once. She stood there and waved as long as she could see the car. She wondered if she would ever see Joe again, and she began to weep.

"Can I help you, Miss Sue?" came the tender voice of Slim. He wondered what all these strange happenings meant. He had not understood why Mr. and Mrs. Norton had disappeared so suddenly. But he wanted to help this young woman whom Joe had left in his charge because she and Joe were his dearest friends on earth.

"No, Slim. There's nothing to do except wait for God to work this out in some miraculous way. I'm going inside now and you go back to bed. If I need you, I'll call."

"I'll be listening and looking," promised Slim.

Sue waited patiently for her lover to return. She did not hear from him at all because there was no way to deliver mail. Many days and nights she spent in prayer. Slim was a faithful watchman. Often at night Sue would hear movement outside, then would come Slim's voice as he endeavored to find out what had made the noise.

However, Sue was not afraid. She only longed for her companion to return safely to her.

The land was desolate. There was but a tiny garden which Slim had planted where he could water it from the deep well. Most of the livestock had been stolen or had died from hunger and thirst. It had rained very little since Joe left. There was not much to eat at the Norton farm, and Sue had heard that people were starving in many areas.

Chapter IV

Five hundred miles north of Winston, a small band of policemen sat in a semi-circle as Joe Norton addressed them. He was a little older now. The lines of his face were deeper, and his face was gaunt and drawn. His voice was clear and carried a note of appreciation to his men, yet it was the voice of authority and leadership.

"Men, the country has ceased from war now because of the drought and famine that are over the land. Hungry men cannot fight. Early tomorrow morning we will start for home. I appreciate your work this past year. You have sacrificed much. May God richly bless you for it all. Thank you and good night." Without another word, he walked to his weather-beaten tent.

Jim Peters and Joe had shared the same tent for the entire time they had been gone. It was an old one with few furnishings. Jim had chosen Joe to be second in command because the men liked and respected him -- a valuable asset in this hour. Of course, Joe had proved himself a worthy leader in all their conflicts. When Joe entered, Jim was sprawled out on his blanket, still awake.

"Well, boy, I've been waiting for you," stated Jim.

"What's up now?"

"Nothing. Only that you have done a splendid job since the night I picked you up. Now it's time for you to return home to that lovely girl who waits patiently for you," replied Jim.

Joe knew most of the men were going home, but he had thought he would have to stay and patrol this area. Though he had been almost unbearably busy since he left home, he had not forgotten the blond-haired girl he had met long ago at Suzie's place in Winston.

"You mean I'm through?" asked Joe.

"Yes. Have everything ready by daylight, take the car, and hit the road. You may have to walk part of the way since there is just a little gas."

"But what are you going to do?"

"There's no reason for me to ever go back to Winston," said Jim sorrowfully.

"Why not, Jim?" questioned Joe.

Jim lay in silence for a time before he answered bitterly. "My wife and our two children were killed and my house burned the night I came for you. Don't ask me any more about it, Joe, because the memory of it is so horrible. I just don't care to go back."

Joe understood Jim's feelings and didn't say another word. He admired the big policeman who had done his duty regardless of circumstances.

Soon Joe was ready to go. He lay on his blanket but couldn't sleep. He could hardly believe he would be with Sue again and they could be happy once more.

Before daylight one morning, Joe was trudging down the road. The Norton farm was just ahead of him. The gasoline that Jim had allotted him had run out twelve miles back. Joe had abandoned the car, as Jim had told him to do, and had walked the rest of the way home. His heart beat faster within his bosom as he turned in the driveway. He was home again! Just as he started to step upon the first step to the porch, a coarse voice came from the corner of the house.

"Don't take another step nearer that house!"

"Slim! You are really on guard, aren't you?" laughed Joe.

"Mister Joe! Mister Joe! How glad I am to see you!" Slim bounded around the house to greet his old friend. His eyes were shining almost as brightly as his few teeth.

"I know a little lady who's gonna be happy now," he exclaimed.

A light was turned on inside the house. Someone unlocked the front door hurriedly. Joe could hardly believe it when the door opened and he saw the silhouette of his beloved Sue. He leaped upon the porch and enfolded her in his arms.

"Joe, darling! I am so glad you're back!" she sobbed upon his shoulder.

"I'm glad to be here, sweet," said Joe, as tears of joy ran down his face and into her hair.

He lifted her in his arms and carried her inside. After locking the door, he sat with her on his lap, clinging to him. They were together again. They were simply too happy to talk.

The days that followed Joe's return were peaceful. He didn't let Sue out of his sight. When he and Slim worked outside, she sat on a nail keg or an apple crate close by. This pleased Joe, for they had been apart for so long. And each realized that they might be separated again at any moment.

Sue had aged somewhat. Worry, sleepless nights, improper diet, and general circumstances had deepened the lines of her face. Her eyes looked hollow, and dark shadows encircled them. Yet she was still a beautiful woman. She talked constantly about God, and she prayed many times a day.

Joe had also changed. He was more mature. His muscles were firm and his countenance set in grim determination. Sue was afraid the time away had hardened him -- not toward her, but toward life in general. Though Joe joined her when she prayed, something seemed amiss in his life.

"We had hope before the rapture, darling. Now we can only expect the worst," said Sue.

"I guess you're right. This torment increases every day. The reason we are not in the thick of it is because of your prayers."

"And your prayers help, too, Joe."

"I don't know, Sue. I used to feel good when I prayed. But now I have no spirit of prayer. I don't know what is wrong with me," confessed Joe.

Sue moved closer to him, and continued, "That is the spirit of the day we live in, Joe. I don't feel as much an urge to pray as I did several months ago. But God does hear us, and we must not fail Him, even if we have to die. The end of everything is close at hand, and the only hope of life is in Christ. Please, dear, keep looking up. He will care for us."

"I surely hope we can escape further disaster, Sue. I would hate to see you killed, even for Christ."

"If it comes to that, and I feel it will, then I have no other choice. I have purposed in my heart that I will not be swallowed up in hell, and you must do the same. I couldn't bear knowing that you were lost."

Joe gazed into space. How many times he had wished he had not been negligent of God's will. Yet it was too late to wish for that. "I'll never have that opportunity again."

"What did you say, dear?" asked Sue. Joe was unaware that he spoke aloud.

"Oh, I was just thinking that I wish we had both been taken in the rapture."

"Well, we missed it. Now we must make the best of it and be true to God. He will deliver us in the way that He sees fit," stated Sue.

Joe started to speak, then stopped. His mouth remained open. His eyes stared at the front door. Slowly the knob turned and someone pushed gently on the door. It was locked. Sue followed Joe's gaze and saw the knob turn again. She dared not even whisper.

Joe pushed a switch on the lamp near them and threw the house into darkness. His hand reached for the 9M Browning automatic close by. He stood, pulled Sue up after him, kissed her brow, then pushed her gently behind the chair. She sat on the floor, expecting the house to be riddled with bullets. Her heart pounded as she prayed earnestly to God.

Joe walked softly across the room and crouched behind another chair. If his voice caused the man or men outside to shoot, he did not want Sue to be in the line of fire. He crouched behind the chair, gun in hand. His nerves were calm and his intentions as grim as death itself.

"Who's out there?" he yelled, shattering the stillness of the night.

"Is that you, Joe Norton?" asked a hoarse voice.

"Maybe," replied Joe. "What can I do for you?"

"You killed our brothers in Jasmine County, and we have come to deal with you. We are five in number, and we mean business. Come out or we'll set this house on fire."

"If I ever killed a man, it was because I had to kill him. And if I kill five more tonight, it will be for the same reason. You men get off my property before I do come out."

Joe's answer carried not the least hint of fear. He was ready to meet the situation.

"You heard what the boss said! Git gone!" Joe heard Slim's voice from the corner of the house, clear and distinct. Slim had an automatic shotgun leveled at the five men who stood on the porch. Because of the blackness of the night, the men could only see the form of a man, half revealed from behind the house. Joe heard Sue whisper, "Thank God!" and he was thankful, too.

Joe slipped quietly and quickly toward the door. He heard one of the men order "Kill that Negro!"

A pistol was fired from the porch, then the dull roar of a shotgun pierced the night twice. Joe saw the streak of fire as he jerked the door open. He heard screams of agony.

Two men fell heavily to the floor. The other three were running down the driveway. Joe fired twice from the edge of the porch. Another man screamed and fell, dead before he hit the ground. Joe and Slim followed the remaining two for a bit, until Joe remembered Sue alone at the house and turned back.

"Get those dead bodies out of the way, Slim. I thank you a lot for showing up at the right time," said Joe, as he slapped Slim's shoulder gratefully.

"It was only my duty, sir. And if they come back, I'll shoot first and give orders second."

"I don't think we'll be bothered with them again, Slim."

"Are you all right?" asked Sue, as Joe entered the house and locked the door again.

"As far as I know, honey. Well, I guess they have found me, and we'll be bothered constantly with men such as they. Let's try to get some sleep now."

Sue wondered how he could be so calm when three men had just been killed. She didn't understand, but she knew God had protected them from death again.

Three weeks later, Joe got out of bed and looked out the window as he always did upon arising. "Sue, darling, get up! It's raining down fire!" he shrieked.

Sue jumped out of bed and looked through the curtains. "My, my! This is a part of it all, Joe. It's a mixture of stuff."

Joe ran out, half dressed, but once on the porch, he dared go no further. Trees were burning, and all the grass and herbs that he could see were on fire. Yet it was no hotter than usual. He examined the falling mixture more closely and discovered there were chunks of ice in the fire, as well as something wet. "It's hailing, too, Sue!"

Sue looked at the sky mingled with black and red. She heard the roaring noise of the storm, as she looked intently at the falling particles.

"Sue, is this the time for the world to burn?" asked Joe.

"No, dear. That is a mixture of hail and fire, mingled with blood. It will burn all the green grass and a third part of all the green trees," she advised.

"Well, it is doing a good job of it. Let's get back inside."

The storm continued to beat upon the earth for five days. Joe and Sue stayed inside, and this became quite irritating to Joe. Sue read her Bible much of the time.

He paced the floor and often asked, "How much longer will this last?"

"I don't know, dear. I hope not much longer, or we won't have a thing to eat," replied Sue.

"I don't feel like I'll ever want to eat again," grumbled Joe.

After the storm ceased, it was three days before Joe could go outside. When he did, he found a soggy muck on the ground, three to four inches deep. "What a mess," he thought, then he was reminded that he was paying for his coldness in God's work which had caused him to miss the rapture. As he walked toward Slim's cabin, he muttered, "If I hadn't been so stupid, I could have missed all this. I could have been with Christ and Mother and Dad and Ann right now."

Joe called to Slim and the old Negro opened the cabin door. "Mister Joe, what in the world has been happening?"

"It's been raining something besides water, Slim."

"These are bad days to be living," Slim muttered, shaking his head. He stepped outside and looked into the overcast sky.

"I'm going to try to find something to eat. You watch after things around here again until I get back," requested Joe.

"Yes, sir. You don't know where you'll have to go, do you?"

"No, but I've got to find something. Slim, is there any fuel for the tractor?"

"Yes, sir. It's got a full tank."

"The ground is such a mess that I'll have to take it," advised Joe.

He returned late that evening with a big supply of groceries. It was not the finest quality of food, but it was food. And they were about to be in dire need. For the eight days they had been stranded, they had hardly had enough food to keep one person strong. Sue had given most of it to Joe and now she was very hungry.

"Well, we will eat for a while," remarked Joe as he and Slim carried in the groceries. "We must be careful with this, dear, for it may be the last we can get for a long while."

"Yes, I understand." Sue sighed.

Soon Sue was preparing a meal for the three of them. Joe sat at the table and they talked as she worked. "Did you have a hard day, Joe?"

"Not too bad. I had to go to old Sam's store to get the food. There's nothing left in the little towns."

"It's just the mercies of God that you found anything."

"Yes, I suppose. We would have starved if I hadn't. I heard that in some places mothers have boiled their children and eaten them," advised Joe.

"Oh, my!" exclaimed Sue. "I believe I'd rather die than eat my own baby."

"You never know what you'll do until the time comes, though. If I hadn't found some food today, we might have been doing something like that."

"Yes, you are right. I hope this food will last us a long time."

Joe stated, "I got all that Sam had except some items that he kept for himself. Oh, I heard something else today, too."

"What's that?" asked Sue anxiously.

"They say the oceans are turning to blood. Sam told me that on the West Coast there was almost nothing but blood being brought in by the tide. They say everything in the water is dying and is being rolled to shore."

"Oh, that is so terrible," groaned Sue.

"The people are moving inland. They can't stand it."

"It is another prophecy being fulfilled, Joe. I don't believe we will have to stay here much longer," commented Sue, as she placed food on a plate for Slim.

"I'll carry that to Slim," offered Joe.

After they ate their meal, Joe turned on the television. The news reports confirmed the rumors. Oceans were indeed turning to blood, and all the marine life was dying. He reflected to himself that he didn't see how the situation could get any worse. But Sue warned him that worse circumstances were ahead. After the good meal, they had a restful night's sleep. When they awoke, Sue exclaimed, "My, what an awful dream!"

Joe yawned, "What was it?"

"I dreamed that we had a little baby, and I was about to boil it for us to eat. Oh, I hope that doesn't happen to another mother. It is so dreadful!"

Joe pulled Sue close to him and stroked her blond hair. "I feel much better today," he said.

"So do I. Food and sleep certainly help a person's feelings."

"I wish I had a million years to spend with you, Sue," Joe whispered tenderly.

"You're sweet. I hope we go to a place where time will never end."

"Mister Joe." It was the voice of Slim.

"Yes," answered Joe, sitting up quickly on the bed.

"I'm gonna walk across the pasture and check on Aunt Rose. I'll be back before too long," advised Slim.

"Okay, Slim. Tell her we said 'hello.'"

Aunt Rose was an old Negro woman who had worked for the Nortons many years ago. They had given her a small cabin, and she still lived there. She and Slim had been lifelong friends.

"Cold weather is on the way," said Joe, looking out the window.

"Yes, I'm a little chilly," remarked Sue.

"Honey, you aren't cold. You just want me to help you up," grinned Joe, as he lifted her in his arms.

"You'd better put me down, big guy," laughed Sue.

Joe paraded through the house and threatened to take her outside in her nightgown. "You can't, Joe! Someone may be out there!"

They carried on playfully until Joe returned to the bedroom, kissed her affectionately, and set her down.

"My, you are rough," sighed Sue.

"Well, don't you like it, beautiful?" laughed Joe.

"More than anything else on earth."

Joe and Sue were busy around the house all day. Slim did not return for lunch, and by late afternoon, Joe was worried about him. "I cannot imagine why he's not back."

"Maybe we should go see about him. Aunt Rose may be sick or something like that," suggested Sue.

"Do you feel like walking that far with me?" asked Joe.

"I'm good for anything if you're along."

They locked the house and started arm-in-arm across the pasture. There was nothing but parched dirt beneath their feet. Joe suggested, "Let's walk over to the big spring and get a drink of water. It's the best water in the country."

"Okay. I am a bit thirsty," agreed Sue.

They walked happily over the little rise. Just before they reached the spring, they stopped in amazement. Their laughter ceased, Joe caught a sharp breath, and Sue clutched his arm. Halfway between them and the spring lay the lifeless form of Slim.

Joe studied the scorched woods before them. It seemed to him that Slim had gone to the spring and started away. Apparently, he had dragged himself ten or fifteen feet, then had given up. Joe and Sue walked to the body. Joe turned him over on his back and examined him carefully. There was no sign of a bullet or a knife wound. Slim had started to swell slightly, but neither Joe nor Sue could tell how he died.

"He could have had a heart attack," offered Sue.

"I guess that's what happened because there's no sign of violence, no marks on his body, and no blood on the ground," he agreed.

"Let's go back to the house, and I'll get a pick and shovel and bury him before dark," said Joe.

Sue turned from the scene and started back over the rise.

"Wait a minute, honey. We came after a drink of water. Don't you want some?" asked Joe.

"No, dear. You get a drink and then we'll go."

She watched Joe go to the spring, kneel down, and start to drink. Then she screamed at the top of her voice and ran down the trail past Slim's body to Joe's side. At her scream, he leaped to his feet and stood trembling, as he gazed at his wife.

"You . . . you didn't drink any water, did you, Joe?" she gasped.

"No, dear. What's wrong with you?"

"Do you see that dead bird down the way?" she said as she pointed downstream a short distance where a dead sparrow lay beside the sparkling spring.

"Yes, I see it."

"This water is poisoned, Joe. The Bible tells about this. Slim got some water here, and it was so poisonous that he only made it that far. The little bird didn't even get away from the stream. Oh, Joe, you came so close! Thank God that I stopped you in time." She leaned on Joe's arm and sobbed. Joe felt sick as he looked from the dead bird to Slim's lifeless form. He could almost feel himself choking and dying from the poisoned water he had come so close to drinking.

"You saved my life again, Sue. In another second, I would have been drinking."

"I imagine one swallow of that water would kill you." She continued to tremble.

"Does this mean that all water is poisoned now?" questioned Joe.

"No, only a third part of it. Let's hope God has allowed ours to remain sweet."

As they started home, Joe looked across the way and saw the top of Aunt Rose's cabin. Perched on the peak of the roof were three huge blackbirds. He turned Sue in that direction and said, "Look. Buzzards are sitting on Aunt Rose's house."

"Oh, my. That's a sign of the worst," whispered Sue.

"I've got to see about her. Do you want to go with me?"

"I'm ready," she boldly asserted.

Joe lifted Sue over the fence, leaped over himself, and they walked rapidly to the cabin. He left Sue at the steps and pushed the front door open. He took one glance inside and quickly closed the door. When he turned to Sue, he was chalk white, sick from the sight he had seen. Aunt Rose's body was stretched on the floor, dead. Hundreds of rats had scurried away from the corpse when Joe had opened the door. The old Negro woman was half eaten by the filthy rodents already. The scent was so strong that Joe was afraid he would collapse.

"Let's go home, honey," he took Sue's hand and walked away from the house. Sue didn't ask Joe even one question. She knew Aunt Rose was dead, possibly from starvation during the eight days of seclusion due to the storm. Sue looked toward the heavens and wondered when their time would come. She knew one of them had to be next. She prayed that it might be herself, for she felt she was not strong enough to see Joe dead or to be separated from him.

She held a light for Joe while he dug a shallow grave and placed Slim's body in it. Sue prayed a simple prayer, then Joe covered the body.

The next morning Joe returned to Aunt Rose's cabin and burned it to the ground. As he watched the flames leap into the sky, he was haunted by the sight of the old Negro woman's body on the floor, half consumed by the rats. What a despicable death she must have suffered! Yet what a horrible time to be living!

That afternoon he caught a bird and poured water from their well into its mouth. The bird swallowed and then drank more. After five minutes, Joe released it, and he and Sue watched it fly away. They both sighed in relief as the bird soared out of sight.

"God has spared us," whispered Sue.

The month following Slim's death was extremely lonely at the Norton farm. The earth was filled with confusion and fear. There were five earthquakes in the area, and it was reported that the earth trembled somewhere almost all the time. There was no decent structure left standing on the farm except the main house, and even it had suffered damage. The sky remained a dull gray and the sun had not shone in many days. Neither the moon nor stars had been seen by human eyes. Then when the sky partially cleared, the whole earth was thrown into turmoil. Strange objects appeared in the sky. One third of the sun had been torn away and refused to shine. A third of the moon was gone, and the remainder looked like a huge container of blood with some invisible power pouring it upon the earth. Only a few stars shone sadly through the mist.

Joe and Sue stayed close to the house, and Joe was often seized with fear. Sue's unwavering faith in God kept her as calm as ever. Whatever God decided to do with her life now suited her just fine. She tried to encourage Joe and talked to him often about God to keep him from committing suicide. She was afraid his faith was not strong enough to sustain him through the days to come.

One day as they sat in the living room reading some reports Joe had picked up in town, Sue said, "Joe, I have something to tell you."

"Okay, honey. Let's hear it."

"Well, I don't think it's such good news. I've been worried about it, but I can't keep it from you any longer."

"What is it, darling?" he asked eagerly, looking at her sad face.

"We are going to have a baby," she spoke in a low voice.

Her words echoed like thunder in Joe's ears. Again he felt sick. Before the rapture this would have been the most wonderful news Sue could have brought him. But now, oh, no! Surely it couldn't be! He couldn't bear the idea of bringing a child into such a world. He arose and began to pace the floor.

"Surely it can't be that, Sue."

"It is, darling. Everything points to it, and I know it's true."

"What will we do?"

"There is nothing we can do except pray that I will be able to deliver the child, that it will be normal, and then dedicate it to God. He has given us this child, and I know He will do the best in all things." Sue spoke without fear.

Joe pulled her into his arms and hot tears poured down his cheeks. "Oh, Sue, I've caused you enough trouble already without this, too. Why doesn't God just smite me and let me die?"

"Don't say that, Joe. You haven't caused me sorrow. I love you, and I know God will see me through this." There was no longer a hospital. Most of the doctors had been killed, and the rest had hidden.

Joe continued to worry, but God had relieved Sue of her burden. It bothered Sue that Joe could not find the same comfort that she had found.

One day as they sat at their noonday meal, the sky began to darken. Joe went outside and looked into the heavens. In the east a dark smoke was boiling out of the horizon and was covering the entire earth. Sue joined Joe and they stood until it was so dark they had to feel their way back inside the house.

"I've never seen it this dark in the middle of the day," wondered Joe, turning on a light.

"It's just another dark moment of the tribulation," advised Sue.

It was late when they retired. The smoke still covered the earth, and they wondered if the morrow would be another dark day. If they had only known what the next day held, neither would have wanted to awaken.

When they rose the next morning, it was light but they heard a terrible roar. Joe dressed quickly and ran outside. Thousands of bugs were flying wildly in the air. He stood amazed. He had never seen such horrible creatures. Suddenly, something touched Joe at the back of his neck. He turned and slapped his neck at the same time. But he was too late. One of the monsters had buried its stinger just above his shirt collar. Joe killed the thing, but oh, what pain! He screamed in agony, and Sue came running out of the house, "What's the matter?"

Before he could answer, one of the monsters landed on Sue's shoulder, raised its stinger to drive it deep into her flesh, then seemed to decide differently. It lowered its stinger, leaped from her shoulder, and was gone.

Joe was holding his neck while examining the creature that had stung him. It looked like a horse ready for battle, with hair like a woman, a face like a man, and teeth like a lion. A long stinger was in its tail, and part of this had broken off in Joe's neck. He looked at Sue. "I will surely die. I have never hurt like this."

She could hardly hear him because of the roar of the flying locusts, so she motioned him to come inside.

"Sue, I'm going to die and leave you," he moaned as he fell across the bed.

"No, dear. You are not going to die, but I am afraid you will be sick for five months. The Bible tells us about this, too."

"I'd rather be dead than feel like this for five months," he groaned and writhed in pain.

The insects left as quickly as they had arrived. Late that evening the noise was gone. Almost every person on earth had felt the fiery sting of one of them. They cried for relief, but no relief came. Joe was among that number, rolling and tossing on his bed, wishing he could die. But death would not come.

Only a few people like Sue, who had God in their hearts, had not felt the sting of the monsters. This was nerve-racking to Sue. But she never complained. Her chief worry was that Joe must not be close to God. She tried to believe that he was, because he had been so good to her, but something inside her told her Joe needed God.

For three years, death had plagued the earth. People had died so fast their bodies were left in the streets and alleys. But now, death refused to bring relief to the tortured.

During the second month after he was stung, Joe tried to kill himself. But his hands were so swollen that he could not grip the handle of his pistol. He begged Sue to give him poison, but she only smiled at him and prayed. She longed to share some of his pain, but could not. He clawed his body until it became a bloody sore. His fever was so high that almost all the hair shed from his body. His hands and feet swelled until they cracked open. Day after day, Sue tenderly bandaged them.

"Another month to go," Sue told herself, then returned to Joe's bedside where she had remained for four months.

Joe became so weak he could not even struggle in his pain. If only he had followed Sue's example and lived close to God. He had wanted to do right, but in almost everything, he had been a little too late.

Five months to the day that the locusts had swarmed, Joe's pain was relieved. His fever cooled and the swelling ceased. Thousands of people were instantly relieved on this day. Then a plague of death swept the land. Men and women were so weak from the physical torture and illness that they could not recover. There had been so much pressure on hearts and nervous systems that when relief came, many could not stand the shock. Almost a third of the population died within a week after the locusts left. Many others were afflicted for the rest of their lives. Life on earth was terrible. None of the remaining farmers planted a crop. There were no longer any grocery stores because the owners had been tormented by the locusts. Besides, there was no food to put in the stores.

After Joe's pain left, he was unconscious for seven days. He was weak because he had eaten so little. It seemed he would die, in spite of Sue's efforts. But her prayers and her skilled hands finally brought him around on the eighth day. She had been beside him day and night, rubbing his limbs, forcing food down his throat, keeping cool towels on his forehead. And the strain was telling on her. She was weary and longed for rest. She had paid dearly for missing the rapture.

Joe opened his eyes and stared at the ceiling. Sue whispered in his ear, "Darling, can you hear me?"

"Yes," he whispered. His lips were thick and parched, and his face thin and wrinkled. It would be a long time before he recovered fully from the past five months, if indeed there were that much time left for earth's inhabitants.

In two weeks, he could walk a bit. He was far from the picture of health, and almost all his hair had fallen out, leaving him bald. He walked over the farm, wanting to pray, but unable to do so. "Oh, if only I could feel the spirit of prayer as I once did."

Not even Sue felt a great desire to pray. But she prayed because she felt it necessary to escape the judgments of hell.

During the first week that Joe was up, Sue rested. She stayed in bed most of the time, but her body was in the clasp of torture. The lack of food weighed heavily on her. Joe's spiritual condition also worried her constantly. She was more interested in his future than in her own. She felt sure God would deliver her in due time. When Joe was out, she wept over the present conditions. She sometimes wondered if she were losing her mind. She prayed earnestly that God would take her out of this world before He allowed that to happen. She worried also about the baby. It was due in a couple of months and she had received no attention, had had very little to eat, and had worked hard during the months she had carried the child. It would break her heart if the baby were not normal, yet she wondered how it could be normal under such circumstances. Her health was breaking fast and now she looked old, tired, and haggard. Yet she never complained.

As Joe regained his strength, he helped Sue around the house. One day as he was outside, Sue lay on her bed and prayed, "God, this burden for Joe is more than I can bear. I know You are able to take it from me. And if I have truly committed him into Your hands, why should I worry? I haven't trusted You with his life as I should, Lord, but now I must have help. Give me strength to bear the load upon my shoulders. Take care of Joe, Lord. I feel that soon You will lead me out of all my sorrow." She prayed a long time, then was relieved of her worry.

As the days passed, Joe waited on Sue as patiently and kindly as he knew how. He had tried to get a doctor for her, but there was none available. Her strength was gone, and she stayed in bed most of the time. She talked very little, but only waited for God's Providence to lead them to a brighter future some day.

During these days, the earth was so poverty stricken that governments became concerned. It didn't matter how much money a man had, there was no food to buy. The entire population was undernourished. Joe and Sue were still living on the supply of groceries he had gotten from Sam, and it was now very meager.

One day in early fall, they heard on television that representatives from every nation were meeting at sea to try to solve the world problems. Joe kept up with this news, but it concerned Sue very little. She seldom turned the television on because she was far more interested in another world than in this one. Her love for Joe had been somewhat crushed by the mean events of the past forty-two months. She still had a burden for his soul, but she looked upon him now more with pity than love. Her affections had been turned entirely upon God.

This didn't bother Joe. He still loved Sue and did all he could for her, but something had gone out of his life. He was more concerned about the matters of the earth and continually sought a way to provide for himself. A month ago, he had stayed close by Sue and would have protected her with his life. Now he stayed away most of the time. When he came in late at night, Sue would ask where he had been. He would shrug and say "To see how things are going."

There was not only a crisis in the world, but there was a crisis in this once happy home. However, neither worried too much about it. She was too sick and had devoted herself to God. She knew the powers of Satan were increasing. She purposed in her heart that she would not be carried into hell now. "I must see Heaven and talk with Christ," she would often say to herself.

Joe let his mind sweep down a different channel and forgot about affairs at home. Sometimes he would try to start a quarrel with Sue, but she never entered into a dispute. Once he threatened to kill her in a rage, but she only smiled and said, "Dearest, death would be the sweetest blessing I could ask for now." Her reaction shocked him. He apologized and left the house. As she watched him go with tears in her eyes, she asked, "Oh, why did Joe give himself to the bad?"

Three weeks later, the conferences at sea concluded. The results were broadcast on television and radio and transmitted over the Internet. In one week's time, a new economic plan was to be enacted over the entire earth. The representatives had appointed a man to rule the earth. He would build his palace and set up his throne somewhere in the ancient world. Everyone would work for him. All foodstuffs would be brought into his storehouses. Ten leading nations would rule under him. All those who followed and supported him would have a seal stamped into their foreheads. If they carried out his orders, they would receive provisions. If not, they would be put to death. It was to be a harsh dictatorship, ruling with mercy those who accepted the worldwide program, and ruling with cruelty those who opposed it.

Men were soon appointed to honorable positions in this new empire. Every town was to have an office where people would receive the mark. They had to first complete a form, signing all their possessions over to the empire. Many men were sent in pairs from headquarters to visit every home on earth. They were to take a census, pass out the forms, then report back to headquarters.

Late one afternoon when Joe had finished his chores, he stood in the front yard scanning the sky. "It will snow before the week is over."

"Oh, I hope not. We don't have much fuel, and the baby will come soon," replied Sue.

The sky was overcast, and a soft wind blew from the west. The clouds raced across the heavens as if fleeing from some unseen monster. The sun had set, leaving a red tinge in the sky. Darkness was creeping over this part of the earth. Sue shuddered and turned to go inside.

As Joe started to follow her, he noticed a car approaching. "My, where did anyone get enough gas to power a car?" he wondered.

The long, black car stopped in front of the house. Two well-dressed men stepped out and one said, "Good evening, sir."

Joe's hand touched his pistol as every muscle in his body sprang to attention. He answered, "Good evening. Do you come in peace?"

"We are sent from the king to discuss business with you that will help the world situation."

Joe released his hold on the gun. "Okay. Come inside."

They walked into the lighted room where Sue sat sewing on a tiny baby dress.

"Good evening," greeted the taller man.

"Good evening," Sue responded courteously.

As the men were seating themselves, Joe recognized them. These were the two inspectors sent from the government to his store years ago to collect several thousand dollars he owed them. What were their names? He couldn't recall, so he glanced at the business cards they had handed him. Ah, yes . . . Longmeyer and Talcott. He opened his mouth to remind them of this acquaintance, then felt a prick of fear in his heart. He decided not to mention this past encounter. Their faces were even harder now than they had been that long-ago day.

Talcott explained to Joe and Sue the program of the new regime. They were to sign the house, the farm, and their lives to the king. He finished by saying, "Here are the forms which you must complete and present at the king's office in town tomorrow. You will have a small seal placed in your forehead and will be given provisions. From then on, you may obtain supplies by right of this mark of the king."

"What if we don't fill out these forms and receive the mark?" asked Joe.

The man's countenance changed. He blinked his eyes several times. "Well, you can't get any provisions.

If you survive three months, death will be pronounced upon you by the king."

He handed a form to Joe, who stretched out his hand to take it.

"Don't take it, Joe!" screamed Sue.

They had all rather ignored Sue, but now three pairs of eyes turned toward her. Her face was pale but defiant, and her eyes glistened with unshed tears.

"I don't have any choice, if I want to live," answered Joe, as he accepted the form. Longmeyer turned to give a form to Sue, but she leaped to her feet.

"I will never accept anything from the devil!" Her lips were now drawn tight, and her nostrils flared with anger. She stood as a wild beast and her eyes were like penetrating fire. "The God I serve will never allow me to do this. And He will provide a way out of this, even if it is death."

"I notice, lady, that you're expecting a child. How long before it will be born?" asked Longmeyer.

"That is none of your business," snapped Sue.

The man's anger was beginning to rise. "When it does come, you will have no doctor. Then you and your baby will die at the decree of the king."

"The baby can be born without a doctor. And if we die, we die in peace. My soul is all I have to save, and never will I sell it to hell!" Sue responded with indignation.

"I'll bring her along tomorrow," Joe told the men, apologizing for his wife's actions.

"No. The king doesn't force anyone to accept his mark. He only makes them wish that they had." Longmeyer had a smirk on his face as he pulled a small computer from his briefcase and entered some information into it. If Sue could have seen what he typed in, she would have had a glimpse of her future.

"We will see you tomorrow," said Talcott to Joe. "And we will see you again, also," he sneered at Sue.

Joe followed them outside, apologizing again, then returned. "I don't see why you couldn't treat our company nice."

"Joe, we can't treat the devil nice. You tried, and when you did, you sold him your soul."

He glared at Sue and started to retort. But something in the blue eyes told him there was no use to argue. He sat down and began to complete his form. Sue retreated to the bedroom for a night of prayer and tears.

Joe was up early the next morning. He ate a handful of parched corn and a meatskin. He wished for something tasty and filling to eat. "Well, maybe after today I can give my stomach a real meal."

He looked through the open door at Sue who lay on the bed. She had not changed into her nightgown. Though Joe knew she had spent a sleepless night, she now slumbered like a baby. He studied her face, wrinkled and drawn from the hardships she had suffered. His gaze rested tenderly on her swollen figure. The pregnancy had been hard on her, and he wished for some way to make her life easier. He knew her real character and her principles had not changed since the day he first met her. He wanted to awaken her and tell her how sorry he was for mistreating her and how much he truly loved and appreciated her. He took a step toward her, hesitated, then turned away.

As Joe left the house, he clutched his form as though it was his life. Every bird sang a mournful song "Go back home, Joe. Don't do it, Joe." But he refused to listen. He told himself this was the only way, and that maybe he could even help Sue and the baby. The north wind blew briskly upon his cheeks, as though chastising him for what he was about to do. But he didn't heed the whiplashes of Mother Nature, either. He pulled his hat lower, turned up his jacket collar, and walked a little faster. Some evil power drove him to the king's office. He closed his eyes to the wind, and a vision of Sue's pleading face loomed before him. "Don't do it, dear. I cannot bear it if you do -- I love you too much."

He looked around quickly. Surely Sue had spoken to him, but he saw no one. "I must be going crazy," he muttered. Half a mile further, her face was again before him, this time just as set and determined as he had seen it last night. She spoke solemnly, "Let me die in peace, for I shall never sell my soul to hell." Joe shuddered and clenched a fist in fear. His other hand was on his gun.

"A man has to take care of himself, and this is the only way to survive," he reasoned. He looked into the sky where even the black clouds seemed to say, "Go back home if you really want to live." His heart pounded, and he wished he could talk this over with his sister Ann. And he needed his dad's guidance in this hour. The tender voice of his mother would mean so much to him now. And where was Sue? He longed for her embrace and prayerful counsel. He knew she would rejoice and welcome him if he returned. But he had mistreated her so that he was ashamed to go back to her. Confusion beat upon him with each step that he took.

Winston wasn't what it used to be. Only three buildings stood. The smallest one was used as the king's office. Here three men were pressing small electric branding irons into the foreheads of the people after they submitted their forms to a woman behind a desk. Women screamed as they received the mark that branded them as followers of the king. Men groaned deeply and unnaturally as the hot metal touched their skin.

Joe stepped into the middle line. He knew almost everyone around him, but he spoke to no one. Even though the weather was cold, his body was wet with perspiration. The battle between life and death inside him had left him exhausted. But he had chosen to live, at least a little while, for the king. He was aghast as he neared the front of the line and saw that such antiquated branding irons were being used to burn the number of the king into the foreheads of the people. Now he understood the screams he had heard as he entered the building. He realized the putrid odor that burned his nostrils was that of burning flesh. He cursed himself for assuming the king's agents would use some painless method to apply the mark – perhaps a laser and invisible ink. It had never occurred to him that the citizens of Winston would be treated like cattle – herded through a line, branded, then shoved aside with no thought for the resultant physical pain. He realized now that the king's empire was going to be far crueler and more oppressive than he had been led to believe. But what was a guy to do, if he wanted to survive? And a spirit within him always forced him to do whatever was necessary to sustain this earthly life.

When Joe's turn came, a heavy man with a cruel gaze instructed him to place his right hand over his heart and repeat after him, "I gladly become a follower of the great king. I will be faithful and loyal to discharge all duties that befall me from his office. I willingly surrender to him all my possessions and my life forever."

Joe's voice was weak as he finished the pledge. To his chagrin, his hand trembled as he passed the form across the desk. He wanted to be macho and pretend this process had no effect upon him. He turned to the young man that held the hot metal in his hand. "Hold tightly to this bar and close your eyes." Joe felt the heat as the iron approached his face. He heard the sizzle of frying flesh, and the fiery pain that accompanied the sound told him it was his own flesh. Fire ran through his body, his heart melted, and his soul was seared. Hatred flared up from his innermost being. Loneliness and darkness gripped him as never before. The iron was removed and someone thrust a card into his hand. "Present this at the next building and your needs will be supplied."

With pain and rage boiling inside him, Joe staggered away blindly. When he showed his card at the next office, he was given a small supply of food which was to last a week. He knew he couldn't help Sue now. This was not enough food for one person.

In the last building, the king's representatives inquired about his farm. He was told that in the spring he would receive the requirements for planting a crop. However, all that he produced would belong to the king and must be brought into his designated storehouse. He was apprised of the severe penalties that would be imposed upon him, and eventually death, if he did not comply.

Joe plodded back home, his body tired and aching. Inside he was cold, hard, and bitter toward everything that lived. Yet a man had to survive. . . .

Three months later, Sue leaned over the bed bathing a tiny baby boy. Little Joseph was born five days after Joe received the mark of the king. Sue had given birth to him all alone about midnight while Joe was away with Jim Peters on some military duty. Jim had persuaded Joe to join the king's army three days after he pledged his loyalty to the king.

Joe came home about once a week. He always brought Sue a little food, but she detected that he was becoming more bitter. He said few words to her and paid no attention to his son. The baby had been sick almost every day of his life. Sue had expected this, considering the lack of care she had suffered before his birth. But now something new had developed in the child. His chest rattled and he was continually coughing and sneezing. She had no thermometer, but she could tell his fever was high and he was growing worse.

As she finished bathing Joseph, she noticed the fire was dying fast. There was only one more piece of wood for tonight. Sue had taken out the gas logs and had pulled boards off the farm buildings for fuel. This open fireplace was her only heat. She could secure no more gas, as she had not received the mark. Joe would not try to get any for her, as some invisible power made him more loyal to the king than to his wife and child.

She placed the last piece of wood on the fire. It crackled and polled and sent forth a radiant heat. She lifted the baby, wrapped him in a woolen blanket, and sat in a rocker near the fire. His body grew hotter and hotter with fever. Sue prayed and wished for daylight, that she might obtain more fuel. She watched as the fire burned low. The blaze went out, then only a bed of coals remained. She pulled her chair closer to the fireplace.

The baby breathed hard and irregularly, too weak to cry. His face was red with fever, and his frail body was racked with pain. Suddenly he lifted his head, opened his weak eyes, and smiled affectionately at her. It seemed he wanted to express appreciation to his faithful mother. Sue stroked his bald head and her heart revived with hope, only to be gripped with fear again. After the baby smiled, he dropped his head, struggled hard in Sue's lap, then lay still. Death had claimed another innocent victim. In the late hour of a cold night, a mother's child was snatched from her bosom and carried far away.

Sue stretched the baby on the bed and tried to revive him. All the skill of her fingers produced not even a sigh from the only sunshine she had known for a long time. After dressing her baby boy in a tiny blue suit she had made for him, Sue sat by the bed, weeping and praying. The north wind howled angrily around the corners of the house. Her body was cold, hungry, tired, and sleepy, but the grief of her soul numbed her body to all things.

Early the next morning, she paced the floor, trying to decide what to do. She had not slept a wink. Joseph lay on the bed in a sheet. She wrapped a blanket around his body and left the house. The ground was frozen, and the wind beat furiously at everything in its path. She went to the garage where Joe once kept his car, placed the baby on the ground, took a spade, and began to dig in the hard earth. The job had to be done and there was no one else to do it. In fact, none of her neighbors would even care about her present circumstances.

When the small grave was finished, Sue read a passage from her Bible. Then she bowed on her knees and prayed long to her God. She lifted her baby's body and placed it gently in the grave. With tears streaming down her face, she covered her child and returned to the house. Exhausted, she fell across the bed, and said, "I am sure the Lord has taken Joseph to live with Him. But what more can happen to me? I have regretted my negligence to the Lord many times." She cried herself into a weary sleep.

Joe came in late that night. Sue greeted him, "Good evening, dear. I'm glad to have you home."

"I'm very tired tonight. Here's a little for you to eat. I cannot bring any more unless you take the mark."

"Then let me starve, Joe, for I'll never accept the king's mark," she spoke firmly.

"Okay. It's your fate, not mine. Where is the baby?"

Sue hesitated, feeling her heart would burst inside her. She looked into the coals upon the hearth, then turned a tearstained face to Joe. "He died in my arms last night with pneumonia."

Joe blinked his eyes and his lips tightened. It was the only trace of pain that he showed. "I guess we are much better off. Well, I've got to leave early, so I'll get to bed." He walked out leaving a lonely wife and mother to seek refuge and consolation where there were none.

About midday, Sue stood inside the garage looking at a small grave. A few wildflowers were placed atop the mound. Every day for almost three months Sue had come to talk to her little boy. Winter was over and summer was coming in full blast. It was a hot, sultry day. Because the garage doors had been used by Sue for fuel during the winter, she saw the car that stopped in front of the house. At first, she thought Joe had come home. She had not seen him in three weeks.

As she came out of the garage, she saw the two men getting out of the long, black car. Her blood ran cold as she recognized them. She wanted to scream and run, but she knew that would not help her. She waited for Longmeyer and Talcott to come to her.

"Good morning," she said, trembling. She had no idea why she was so afraid. She hadn't felt this way in a long time.

"I suppose you know your time is up, and you have not received the king's mark. We are to escort you to his office. Will you go willingly?"

She hesitated, wondering what she should do. Then she spoke, "I shall never go willingly, but if you will give me ten minutes, I will go with you."

"Your request is granted," replied Talcott, looking at his Gucci watch.

Sue turned back into the garage, bowed next to the tiny grave, and prayed softly to her God. "Oh, Lord, this must be the time of my deliverance from the grief of this life. I trust that I have lived right and exalted Your name in the past few years. Give me grace to yet stand for Thee, for I know there is none other like Thee." She rose to her feet, and said, "Well, Joseph, my son, I must leave you now. But if your mother has found favor with the Lord, maybe He will let me hold you in the other world. Be a sweet boy, and always remember that your father is the most wonderful man who ever lived. Goodbye, darling."

Sue choked back scalding tears and walked out of the garage. There was no fear in her now. She had new courage, and the hope of deliverance pounded in her soul.

"Will I need to take anything with me?" she asked the men.

"No. We will furnish everything," coldly replied Longmeyer.

Sue went into the house, picked up a small New Testament and slipped it into her dress. "Wherever I go, let Thy word go with me."

She was taken to the king's office and tried before several officials at three o'clock that afternoon. Talcott and Longmeyer were witnesses against her. No one spoke for her. They gave Sue a final chance to accept the mark or die.

"Let me die for the cause of Jesus Christ, Whom I represent," she said solemnly.

It was decreed and a public announcement made that Sue Norton would be burned at the stake in the square at ten o'clock the next morning. She was locked in a small room where she spent the night, reading the New Testament and praying. Though she had spent far too many sleepless nights, her consolation now was that she would never spend another one. She was not afraid to die.

At ten o'clock the next day, the park was filled with people. News of the upcoming execution had traveled fast, and almost everyone was there to see it. Men laughed and talked in small groups while the women whispered to each other and fussed at the children. Most of them knew Sue, but they only said, "Poor girl. It's a shame she has to be so foolish and not serve the king."

On the south side of the park, a young man stood under the low-hanging boughs of a tree. His eyes were fastened on a large post about six feet tall which had been erected in the center of the square. The man wore a uniform of the king's army, and his helmet was pulled low over his eyes as though he did not wish to be identified. It was Joe Norton. The lines of his face were etched more deeply now, but the strength of a young lion was obvious in his powerful body as he leaned against the tree.

Suddenly a trumpet sounded and the park immediately became quiet. The marching of soldiers was heard in the street. Three guards with drawn pistols appeared at the edge of the park. Following them was a tired, starving woman marching bravely to a fiery stake.

Another guard followed Sue with a gun in his hand. Behind him were three men, all of whom carried wood. Another held a large container of gas. When they arrived at the stake, Sue was forced roughly against it. Then her hands were tied behind the stake and the wood was laid around her feet, almost waist high. The king's executioner stepped up and said, "Do you have any last words to speak for yourself?"

She hesitated only a second before she spoke clearly. "I must say I am terribly sorry that my husband erred in the way and has sentenced himself to hell by receiving the mark of the king. But I cannot forsake the Lord for all His kindness to me. May my last words and actions on this earth be for the glory of the One Who was crucified for me. For if I die for Him, I shall live with Him in a better land."

"Then you are ready to die?" asked the man roughly.

"Yes, I am ready to die for the Christ of Glory." There was not a trace of fear in her face. The executioner stepped back and picked up the gas can.

Joe stood erect, trembling, his hand on the butt of his holstered pistol. Why, oh why, did she have to die such a violent death? Why wouldn't they just give her a lethal injection and let her die alone, without having to be made a public spectacle? Was it necessary that the whole town witness this wonderful Christian being martyred in such a repulsive style of execution? Sue didn't deserve this. It was probably his own negligence that had brought her to such a fate. If she had not loved him so dearly, she would have been in South America in God's perfect will at the time of the rapture, and she would have missed all the tribulation she had suffered. Joe had a strong desire to rush in and rescue the woman who had meant so much to him. Surely there must be some way he could save her, some place they could escape to and find sustenance. He could not bear to think that the lovely body he had held in his arms so many times was about to become no more than a mound of ashes.

His face contorted with emotion, he took a step forward. But Jim Peters touched him on the arm and whispered, "You can't do any good now, Joe." Jim had moved to his side unnoticed, because he had calculated Joe would get himself into trouble trying to help Sue.

Joe cursed under his breath, then a strong feeling of hatred and cruelty swept over him. "If only she hadn't been so foolish. Oh, if only she had taken the mark! But she knew what she was getting herself into when she refused," he muttered. The look he turned upon Jim Peters changed from guilt to helplessness to bitterness, and finally, to hardness.

The man soaked the wood with gasoline, and Joe saw him strike a match to the wood. Flames leaped up angrily, and smoke hid Sue's form for a moment. When she was revealed again, Joe saw her in all the exquisite beauty he had seen when he first met her at Suzie's place. Her face was lifted to Heaven. No more was it tired and drawn. There was a tender smile upon her lips. One more time, Joe wanted to run take her in his arms again, but it was too late now. The man threw more gasoline on the fire. The flames shot up and concealed the beautiful, serene face.

People began to leave the park as the smell of burning flesh filled the air. Soon only a small heap of ashes marked the end of a faithful servant of the Lord. Sue had died without making a sound.

Joe turned away, nauseated to the very core of his being. Now his life would be colder and lonelier than ever. He walked to his quarters and stretched out on the bunk. He lay sleepless, tossing and turning and remembering sweet Sue, for hours.

For three years after Sue's death, the king's army marched in fighting campaigns, killing and conquering all who opposed the king. Every able man had been called into the army. Joe was in Winston only a few days after his wife's death. For a while, he thought often of Sue, then deeds of cruelty crushed all affection in his heart.

One day Joe's group of soldiers boarded a ship and sailed for many days. He knew not where they landed, for he had learned long ago not to ask questions. They waited five days, then were joined by many other soldiers. It was the largest army Joe had ever heard about. He marched on the outside, almost in the front. Joe had never seen the strong man who gave the orders.

For a day and a night they marched without halting. They stopped for a little stale bread and some parched corn. Still more soldiers joined them before they moved on. About mid morning, rain began to fall, yet they marched. Joe moved close to Jim Peters and whispered, "Who is the man that leads us?"

"That's the king," Jim whispered back. They spoke no more for fear of repercussion.

Darkness crept over the horizon. Word was passed that a meal would be eaten and camp made for the night. They were ordered to rest and be ready to march very early the next morning.

Joe ate his stale bread, dried beef, and a small can of beans. Afterwards, he and Jim Peters stretched their tent. Joe rolled himself up in his blanket because the weather was damp and cool. "Where are we going, Jim?"

"I don't know, but we will need some rest. You better get to sleep, boy."

Soon Jim breathed heavily, but Joe could not sleep, although every muscle and bone in his body ached. His mind went to his younger days with his sister Ann. He recalled her devotion to him. He remembered the heart-rending scene at her deathbed, and he wondered if he would ever see her again. He thought of his mom and dad and how much they had invested in him. If only he had Shep Owen or Ben Shank to talk to now. Then he allowed his thoughts to turn to a lovely face, blond hair, and a slim figure. He had once had a faithful wife. Remembrance of her loyalty and devotion, both to him and to her God, caused Joe's heart to soften just a bit. He remembered her agony and torment the last few years of her life, and her continuing love for him. Then he saw her in the square, her face lifted to Heaven from among the flames. Joe clenched his fists and cursed himself again for not rescuing the best woman who had ever lived. Then he remembered his son, Joseph. He could see two tiny hands reaching for him, two little eyes adoring his father, and soft lips parted in a sweet baby smile.

It was more than Joe could bear. He crawled out of the tent and stood. Small fires had been built by the sentries, and they dotted the valley where the army was encamped. This was the largest, most beautiful valley Joe had ever seen. As it stretched northward, it broadened. Green grass lined the basin of the valley, and southward it narrowed just a bit. Several trees grew on the far western bank. Halfway up to the trees, a large rock protruded from the side of the hill. Gray moss fell from the rock, almost touching the ground below. When they had camped the evening before, Joe had thought what a cool place this would be to rest on a hot day.

Unconsciously, he now started in that direction, then checked himself, for he would be killed if found without the camp at night. He looked at the thousands of tents and told himself there was nothing to fear, for an army like this could never fail. He crawled back into the tent he shared with Jim Peters, wrapped himself in his blanket, and slept.

The next morning he slept later than usual. "What time is it?" he asked Jim, who was packing his gear.

"It's about daybreak, and orders have just been given that we will march in ten minutes."

Joe leaped up and began to prepare. In nine minutes, he and Jim had the tent packed and were ready to go. Joe felt something unusual was going to happen today. And he could not shake the memories he had relived the previous night. A little light was coming into the valley now, and he could see the outline of the huge rock. He heard the voice of the king as he issued orders. He strapped on his gun, and stepped in place. He kept his eye on the king, who stood with his hand in the air. When his hand fell, it was the signal to march.

The hand fell, but no one moved except the king and his governor. They took only a couple of steps, then stopped. Just as the signal had been given, a flash of lightning raced across the sky and a peculiar light filled the entire universe. It was brighter than the noonday sun. A loud roar was heard behind them, and every man turned to see what it was.

Riding over the eastern horizon, as though they came out of the sky, was a vast, white-robed army. The Leader of this army sat astride a powerful white stallion. His countenance was as bright as the sun. He wore a flowing, white robe and was girded about with a golden girdle. His eyes were as coals of fire that penetrated the heart of every man in the king's army. A multitude of white-robed people followed Him upon white horses.

Joe stood awestruck, watching the beautiful sight that approached them. His heart pounded within him, and he remembered the teaching of the Bible. "Surely this must be Christ with His army," he whispered in awe to himself.

The Captain came nearer with His multitude. His eyes searched every soul, and Joe could not bear to look at Him. Even when he looked away, he felt those piercing eyes. His brain was in mass confusion, and he grabbed the gun at his side. Men broke rank and Joe heard the firing of guns. The king's army was fighting among themselves. A supernatural power caused them to kill their fellow soldiers.

A soldier rushed upon Joe with a long blade. Joe fired his gun into the man's face and he fell dead. Four more times he fired, then realized his ammunition was gone. Each man had been given only a small supply, and they were to get more today. Joe reached for the long blade strapped to his side. He looked often at the approaching Leader, but each time this resulted in more confusion within him. The clash of weapons, the dull thud of metal striking flesh, the groans of the dying, and the screams of the wounded only added to the frustration of Joe Norton.

It seemed he fought for days. Night did not come, for the brightness of this army drove back the darkness. Joe was tired and hungry, and he sought a place of refuge. Thousands had been slain, and he walked in their blood, almost ankle deep. His eyes fell upon the huge rock he had noted the prior evening. Twice he had wanted to go there, and now he would go. He slipped from the midst of the battle, looking back often to see if anyone had spotted his flight. He ran up the slope to the rock, pushed the moss back, and stepped under the overhang. The moss closed behind him and he found himself in a room-like enclosure. A spring gurgled between two rocks and ran down the slope. Joe realized then why the moss had grown there.

He took a drink of the cool water, then sat down and tried to think clearly. He decided to stay in this small place until the battle was over. Then he would emerge and surrender to Christ. Surely He would be merciful at a time like this. Joe relaxed somewhat and listened to the sounds below him. It seemed he heard the other army singing. He shuddered at the thought of death, then told himself he was safe and closed his eyes for a little rest.

Just as he felt secure, he heard footsteps coming up the slope. He put his hand on his blade and pushed back the moss. Then he put his blade back into its sheath and stepped out to greet Jim Peters. "Come in and rest, fellow."

"You thought you'd get away, did you?" snarled Peters. Joe realized this was a totally different Jim Peters. He was covered with blood, and terror was in his face. His eyes were wild and fierce as he rushed up the slope with his sword in the air. His teeth were bared and his lips curled in a scowl. He struck hard at his young friend.

"What's the matter?" yelled Joe, as he blocked the blow. But the blade struck his forearm and he winced as the steel cut through the flesh and to the bone. Fire burned within him and the desire to live struggled again. If he must kill in order to live, so be it. He reached for his sword.

Peters swung hard at Joe, cursing and swearing. Although he was mad, he was still a good fighter. Joe avoided a second attack, waiting for an opening. When

Jim saw that Joe had stepped aside, he swung from a different angle and the blade dug deep into Joe's side. Joe felt the sting, then with all his might, he thrust his own blade into the unprotected chest of Jim Peters. Peters' hand relaxed upon his sword, his eyes glazed, and he fell upon the rock, foaming at the mouth. He struggled only seconds, then lay still. His blood ran into the little stream, coloring the water that ran down into the valley. Joe's last friend on earth was dead.

He was sick. He looked at Jim's body, then sat down on the soft moss. He tied his belt around his left arm, trying to stop the flow of blood. Then he packed moss into the wound in his side. If only he could stop the loss of blood, then he had hope of living. And surely he must live.

He looked over the valley again. Innumerable dead bodies dotted the earth. The few who yet lived were wounded unto death. Joe looked across at the white-robed army. He saw the Leader get off his horse and walk toward the king. No words were spoken, as far as Joe could tell. They crossed swords, and the white-robed Leader smote the king with one blow of His powerful hand. The king's governor attempted to rush upon the Leader, but he fell across the body of the king and they died together.

Joe's eyes blurred. Blackness threatened to overcome him, but he fought it down. He blinked his eyes, then saw clearly again.

The only activity in the valley now was that of the white-robed army. The Leader was astride his horse again, and they were passing through the valley. They would soon come by Joe. His heart leaped within him when they turned his way. Now he would call to this King, and surely He would help him.

As the army was passing, Joe opened his mouth to hail the great King, but his voice was so weak that no one heard. He called again, but the Leader's face was set straight forward and he did not turn. Joe raised a weak, trembling arm, but it was unheeded. He dropped his arm, and hot tears flowed from his eyes. His only hope of living was passing by. For the first time in his life, Joe was afraid -- afraid to die. Yet some fight was left in him. He dried his eyes and tried to rise to go with the army. But it was no use. His left leg was numb and helpless, and the right leg too weak to support him. His eyes blurred again and he muttered, "I cannot die here! I cannot! If I do, then I shall never go to live with Mother and Dad and Ann and Sue and little Joseph. Oh, I must not disappoint them!"

This thought gave him some added strength, and he struggled in vain to rise again. But he sank back on the moss and leaned against a rock. Only a tiny bit of blood was oozing from his side now. He lifted his eyes and looked at the army once more. Most of it had passed, but maybe he could get someone to look. Suddenly, his heart hammered wildly! Hope revived, and his eyes flashed with new vision. He saw a lovely girl, resplendent in her snow-white robe, riding on the outskirts of the army. He thought . . . then he knew . . . yes, it *was* Sue!

She was far more beautiful than he had ever seen her. There was a glory about her, a radiance that was awe-inspiring. A golden crown was upon her head. Her face was aglow like all the others and was focused on their Leader. But Joe knew that Sue would hear and would help him. She had never refused him anything, and now when he needed her so much, surely she would come to help him.

Joe tried to call to Sue, but his voice failed him. He attempted to raise a weak hand to her, but it lay limply at his side. He was too weak to move even a muscle.

He saw Sue pass by. It seemed that her eyes turned once to look at him. They were filled with sympathy and pity, but she could not help him now. As he watched her ride on with the magnificent multitude, Joe knew this was the last time he would ever see her.

He looked again at the moss-covered rock he had thought to be his refuge and at the body of Jim Peters. He saw that the little stream that had been red with blood was clear again. It had already carried all of Joe's blood to the valley below.

Joe shuddered at the thought of dying, then closed his eyes to this world. The dull roar of hell rushed up after him. The power of death gripped him fiercely. As Joe slipped into a long and terrible eternity, he knew that he was forever *too late*!

THE END